PSYCHO-
LINGUISTICS

"The Language of the Mind!"

By Patrick Kelly Porter, Ph.D
Foreword by Dr. Paul T. Adams

*This book is dedicated to those wishing
to discover the essence of change technology.
May you awaken to the language of your mind.*

ATG Publishing
c\o 309 Aragona Blvd. Ste. 102-712
Virginia Beach, Virginia state
Postal Zone/Code [23462]
804-631-2928
800-880-0436

Other Books & Tapes
By Patrick Porter, Ph.D
Awaken the Genius
Mind Technology for the 21st Century
Passport To Your Child's Genius
How to Awaken the Brilliance in Your Child
Journal into Genius
Workbook Companion to Awaken the Genius
Awaken Your Genius! 4-ProcessTape Sets:
Adventures in Accelerated Learning
Adventures in Self-Discovery
Psycho-Linguistics 4-ProcessTape Set::
Personal Evolution Success! Series
Personal Evolution - Weight Loss!
Personal Evolution - Stop Smoking!
The Power of Your Voice
Transcripts for Personal Evolution

For complete information about Seminars
or for a catalog of self-help books and tapes,
write:
Awaken the Genius Foundation
c\o 309 Aragona Blvd. Ste. #102-712
Virginia Beach, Virginia state
Postal Zone/Code [23462]
800-880-0436
Cover Art: Sam Johnson

First printing: January, 1995

ISBN: 0-9637611-7-X
Library of Congress Card Number: 93-086045
Printed in the united States of America

10 9 8 7 6 5 4 3

Table of Contents

Foreword

It has often been said that *knowledge is power*. The truth is that knowledge *applied* is power. Through Psycho-Linguistics, Dr. Patrick Porter teaches how to apply the power of mind technology. Patrick Porter has often been noted for his ability to take technical, academic jargon into a laymen's language that is not only practical, but usable by people from every walk of life. *Psycho-Linguistics; The Language of the Mind* is perhaps his best display of this skill.

In 1967 I wrote a book called, *The New Self-Hypnosis*. Within its pages I wrote about King Solomon who said, in essence, that the thing which determines human character is not what a man thinks or verbalizes consciously, but what he thinks "in his heart," or subconsciously. "For as a man thinketh in his heart, so is he." (Proverbs 23:7 K.J.V.) Since the days of King Solomon, many discoveries about the mind have confirmed what he said. What you think in your heart, or subconscious, becomes you and this can be either good or bad, depending upon how you created the program. At that time I believed (and still do) that the very best way to reach those subconscious programs was through hypnosis and/or self-hypnosis. That was in 1967.

Today, with Dr. Porter's Psycho-Linguistics, access to the subconscious is easier, more concise and effective than ever before. What Dr. Porter has done in developing Psycho-Linguistics was to blend together the best of hypnosis, visualization and a relatively new science known as Neuro-Linguistic Programming. This is hypnosis at its highest level. He has taken these sciences out of the exclusive domain of academia and into the realm of the practical. Each of these methods has been time-tested for long term success. Dr. Porter and his associates use these techniques on a daily basis in Positive Changes clinics across the country.

Here are tools that can help the seasoned professional or the neophyte. Yet, you must do more than simply read the material presented

i

in Psycho-Linguistics; you must apply the teachings. A unique feature of Psycho-Linguistics is that Dr. Porter doesn't just teach you theories. In addition to the methodology, he gives you word-for-word formulas that you can use immediately. Dr. Porter has indeed written a text you can refer to for the rest of your professional career or personal life. You will read it *and apply it* over and over again.

Paul T. Adams, Ph.D

Acknowledgments

I wish to offer my thanks to the creative force known by some as God, and by others as Divine Mind, for continuous guidance and the motivation to persevere in my educational goals and development as a Counselor.

I wish to give thanks for such a loving family who has supported me through my research and development. Especially my wife Cynthia who has done such a fine job editing the volumes of information that went into the creation of this text. A heartfelt thanks to Professor Alice Adams of Prestonsburg College for her valuable time and effort in editing the text and for her quality suggestions.

I wish to express my thanks to my father, Dr. Michael J. Porter, who started my research in the area of psychology at an early age by teaching me how the power of my mind, through hypnosis and imagery, could transform my life. Special thanks are also due to Dr. Paul T. Adams who allowed me to serve as his apprentice and to develop the skills of Psycho-Linguistics. Additional thanks to Dr. Adams for his thoughtful foreword to this book.

I'm also grateful to the staff of NLP of Arizona and NLP Comprehensive who trained me in the skills of NLP. I give special thanks to the founders of NLP, Richard Bandler and John Grinder, for bringing forth this non-judgmental therapeutic approach that has proven their philosophy time and again that *"Anyone can do anything . . . If one person can do something it is possible to model it and teach it to anyone else."*

I would also like to give thanks to the staff at Light and Sound Research, especially Linnea Reid and Larry Gillen, for allowing me to be a part of the growing field of mind technology. Also special thanks to Jerry DeShazo, who encouraged my research and development as a therapist.

Special appreciation is due the many thousands of clients who have passed through the doors of my center, Positive Changes, and have allowed me to use and expand upon the therapeutic approaches outlined in this text.

I would also like to honor all the *"Networkers"* out there who make this world work with such harmony and consistency. A special thanks to Rita Livingston, who sponsored my work into Barbados, West Indies where I met with Dr. Jim Hurtak who provided me with the inspiration to put my work into the current format.

A special and heartfelt thanks to the reader. It is my hope that one of you will become inspired to write the next exciting mind technology so that I can continue to learn and grow. As a friend of mine, Dr. Gil Gilley, has said, *"When you stop growing you begin to rot!"* May the ground under your feet be fertile soil and the seeds of greatness sprout through your actions. May you benefit from the years of discovery found in this text.

-- Love & Light,

Patrick Porter

Preface

There are, indeed, many abilities of the mind that we as humans have in common. Our minds all process information from a foundation of five primary access systems, better known as our *"senses."* These are visual, auditory, kinesthetic (tactile or emotional feelings), and the senses of smell (olfactory) and taste (gustatory). These five senses help our mind to process the world around us. Many will argue over the existence of a sixth sense. This has been the topic of considerable controversy, although it seems quite logical that when all of the five senses are working together in harmony and forecasting what the probable future will be, it creates in essence a *"sixth sense."*

All of these senses work together to create your perception of reality. This is not to be confused with reality itself, however. Just ask two eyewitnesses, who were at the same event at the exact same time, to describe what they saw, heard and experienced at the scene. Don't be too surprised by the two totally different versions described to you. When touching into the language of the mind you are dealing with perceptions of reality; or an individual's inner map and guideline. These are the guidelines used for that person to achieve personal success. Therefore, success is a state of mind. Through the patterns of *Psycho-Linguistics*, I have spent the last ten years researching how to create that successful state of mind; how and when to use the visual and auditory fields, the emotional responses, and, when appropriate, the gustatory and olfactory senses.

In my early years of practice, one of my greatest challenges came whenever I was asked to explain just how the brain and mind work. I understood it quite well within my own mind, but could never seem to put it into the right descriptive words. And then, the age of the computer dawned and I found myself the perfect analogy to describe the functions of the brain and mind. This is because, just like a computer, you must know the right sequence to access your mind so that the appropriate changes can be made. Once you have found that access the only limits will be the ones you set. If you have ever attempted to learn to run a computer you will know just what I mean. The computer has certain laws that must be followed exactly or it will either do nothing at all or certainly not the function that you wanted it to perform. No matter how frustrated or upset you get, it will simply wait patiently for you to do it by the law. When you finally learn the laws of the computer and follow them to the letter, it will happily and effortlessly perform all of your functions and bring forth the outcome you desire.

So it is with the mind. If you attempt to make changes in your life without ever gaining access to the laws that are the working of your own mind, either nothing at all will happen, or perhaps you will experience an outcome that is much different from the one you had set out to achieve.

My discoveries started at a very early age when I was mastering the art of troublemaking in school. Not coincidentally, at the same time my father was mastering the art of alcohol. We were both much too successful. For my father it paved the way for his discovery of Alcoholics Anonymous, better known as AA. The entire family would go to the meetings, my mother to Alanon and the kids to Alateen. This was often quite a production since there were nine children to load into the car each week. For a time the meetings seemed to bring our family closer together, but AA lacked the staying power we were seeking. Somehow, at least in my father's case, it always seemed to give the alcoholic an out.

Still, it was because of AA that my father was able to experience a shift in his awareness. At one of the meetings an announcement was made about a relaxation seminar that would be offered locally. This seemed to be right up Dad's alley, especially since he couldn't recall a time in his life when he was able to truly relax. It was this seminar that started his research into just what the mind could do for him and for his family. He began to understand that he had the ability, with the use of his mind, to deal with everyday stress, which in turn somehow curbed his desire to drink. From there he discovered the process of Silva Mind Control. His addiction was transformed; he now had a thirst for knowledge, which then developed into the desire to share his learning with others. He became a Silva Instructor and soon advanced to training others.

One of the nice things about having a Silva Mind Control Instructor for a father is that my eight siblings and I became his guinea pigs--which was perfect. We were all soon learning the unlimited potential in putting our fantastic young minds to use. Each of us found different and very individual ways to benefit from each new discovery.

As it must be when knowledge exceeds an occupation, my father became very restless in his job at the local factory. He decided it was time to find an appropriate career. He was quick in ending his ties with the company which had employed him for over fifteen years. His interest soon turned to the area of hypnotherapy. What better way to access that part of the mind where all change needs to start? With Dr. Paul Adams, author of *The New Self Hypnosis*, my father studied and quickly learned the techniques of hypnotherapy. He was soon to realize that the processes of Jose Silva's Mind Control were almost identical to the patterns of hypnosis.

As I came of age and my interest in hypnotherapy grew, I found myself frequenting my father's library to quench my own thirst for more information. I guess it was without even my conscious awareness that I decided to become a therapist myself. During my college years, I joined my father's practice in the small Michigan town which had been my life. After nearly five years, we decided to make the move to a larger metropolis: Phoenix, Arizona. With the help of Dr. Adams, we started our first Positive Changes Center. Phoenix was a whole new world opened up to us. It was here that my father and I attended our first seminar on Neuro-Linguistic Programming (NLP). This seminar, and the training that followed, changed the course of our practice forever. We left the introductory lecture feeling ecstatic. It was during this seminar that we were able to confirm what we had begun to suspect. It takes much more than simply putting someone into a state for a purpose *(the main thrust of most standard hypnosis techniques)*. Much, much more important is knowing the way to present the new information so the bio-computer *(brain)* can truly assimilate it and then feed it back during day-to-day activities as effective and permanent behavior modifications.

I was privileged to have been trained by some of the best NLP instructors in the country. From them I continuously heard talk of a therapist by the name of Milton Erickson. Although Dr. Erickson is no longer with us, luck was with me in that the Ericksonian Institute happened to be located just a few miles from my home in Phoenix. I had a never-ending supply of information on Dr. Erickson and his therapeutic techniques. All my clients were now the recipients of everything I was learning.

During this time I was fortunate to be a part of one of the most successful hypnotherapy practices in the country, with offices in four cities and over 10 therapists using the techniques. It didn't take us long to learn which patterns of change were truly applicable and which ones are only effective for impressing seminar participants.

I have since located my business to Lexington, Kentucky, where I found a receptive community, also in search of ways to better their lives. Before leaving Arizona I was asked to write a program to be used by the Arizona Health Council and the state to re-educate DUI. offenders. In so doing, I seized the opportunity to put my thoughts, techniques and patterns on paper. Thus, the patterns of *Psycho-Linguistics* were born.

It would be virtually impossible to give credit to all of the authors, educators, and trainers who have contributed to the development of these techniques. One thing that you can depend upon is that these methods will continually be modified and enhanced as new client needs are presented to me.

These patterns are not intended to diminish hypnosis, NLP, positive thinking, meditation, mind control, or any other mind technology. Rather, my aim is to share what I have found successful for my clients and myself. There is no superior change technology; I have found profound benefits in each method. We are fortunate to be living in the information age where there are abundant resources available for self-help or for helping others to make changes or improvements to their day-to-day lives. Remember always, *"The law of mind is the law of belief,"* and, of course, *there are no limits to consciousness.*

THE FIRST STEP IS TO BE A MASTER OF COMMUNICATION

"Communication" has been a buzz word in psychology and counseling for several years. How many couples have reported to marriage counselors, "We just don't communicate anymore"? But how many of these couples have ever been taught *how* to communicate? For many, it never occurred to them that they could learn how to access each other's bio-computer; how to speak the language of the other person's mind. They just assumed there was something wrong between them.

In order to have an impact in self-improvement or in helping others, you must first be a master of communication. You will need to know how to access the other person's *(and your own)* bio-computer.

INITIATION

What is

"Psycho-Linguistics?"

Psycho-Linguistic Therapy is designed around processes or strategies rather than problems. A therapist using many standard therapeutic techniques will find it necessary to re-create all of the sensitive information surrounding the experience and then confront the patient on a conscious level, usually reproducing all of the pain and suffering as well. Also, the mechanics of most therapies infer that in some way the problem could have, in most cases, been avoided. Yet the "Big Book" of Alcoholics Anonymous[1] points out that knowledge does not a sure cure make. On every pack of cigarettes the Surgeon General warns that cigarette smoking is hazardous to your health. Yet millions of people, even with the knowledge that each inhalation is destroying their body, will continue to practice the habit without skipping a beat. *Why?* This question is what first inspired me to look into alternative programs and therapies using a more solution-driven approach *(how to become a non-smoker)* rather than a problem driven approach *(why you are a smoker)*.

I wanted to understand what would motivate such curious behavior. This was the answer I was seeking when I began my research. My discoveries during the search are what subsequently inspired the *Psycho-Linguistic* Therapy which I will outline herein.

Psycho-Linguistic therapy bases its results on the truth that we all learn behaviors through life experience and we structure that truth as memories which are stored through the sensory channels. Through the *Psycho-Linguistic* process I will demonstrate how people are able to change their thinking processes and in turn change their lives. The findings are from a basis of hands-on results gathered through research at my Positive Changes clinics in

---

[1]Alcoholics Anonymous World Services, Inc., 3rd Edition, 1976

Louisville and Lexington, Kentucky, Tennessee; Nevada, Oregon, Arizona and Pennsylvania.

Perhaps by reflecting upon the origins of *Psycho-Linguistics*, and then relating just how we developed the patterns, you will begin to get the feel for *what* Psycho-Linguistics is, and hopefully for what deeper meaning it will have in your own search for a **positive change**.

In simplest terms: *Psycho-Linguistics* is a usable, rapid and efficient method for accessing your mind or another individual's mind and making changes to behaviors, attitudes and/or thought patterns. *Psycho-Linguistics* is a combined study and theory of the processes of Neuro-Linguistic Programming (NLP), Hypnosis, Self-Talk, Imagery, and Ericksonian Hypnosis. It is through the use of all of the above methods that I developed *Psycho-Linguistics: The Language of the Mind.*

The results achieved with this technology are based on the impact made to the individual's thinking process, rather than on gaining a greater insight into the person's problems. This is not to suggest that modern psychology does not deal with this issue; it is simply handled in a different way. If it is your wish is to make an impact on your mind or that of another, there is much more involved than simply accessing an altered state *(the premise of hypnosis)*, or even saying the right thing; you need to say it in the right order and in a way that it will be acceptable to that individual's mind. To influence any one mind, it is essential that you communicate in a language with which it can relate. This is where *Psycho-Linguistic* therapy accelerates the process and where my point will be made.

Through extensive research, with real people expressing real *"problems,"* I have come to the conclusion that the *problem* has no relevancy to the *solution*. This can be likened to physical illness in that the symptom is not the disease. If medical doctors treated only symptoms their cure rate would be next to nil. Understand that each person's mind is goal striving and will do its best with whatever information is at hand. In other words, each individual simply needs to discover their unconscious triggers or previous programming and make adjustments, thus allowing a free flow of communication through all channels so that a new and more appropriate choice can be made.

Our minds are designed to create what we are mentally rehearsing. Unfortunately, this is not always what is needed or intended. If the unconscious is convinced that this person is a failure, and has been rehearsing failure through mental movies and continuous re-runs, then the individual will become successful at failure. On the other hand, if a person rehearses success while in an altered state of awareness--not just positive affirmation but a full sensory experience--then change will occur because at that level of thinking the mental rehearsal and the physical action will be stored in equal measure. Through physical and mental rehearsal it will soon come to pass as reality.

One of my main purposes in developing these non-contextual techniques was for use by trainers who want to offer group processing. With *Psycho-Linguistic* training the individual participants are able to audit themselves and make the appropriate changes using the defined outline of procedures. Once learned, the results can be tested, and adjustments can be made on a day-to-day basis. This follows along the same guideline and theory as the Alcoholics Anonymous structure of *"One day at a time."*

"We hold these truths to be sacred & undeniable;
that all men are created equal & independent,
that from that equal creation they derive rights
inherent & inalienable,
among which are the preservation of life,
& liberty, & the pursuit of happiness."

THOMAS JEFFERSON

"The greatest discovery
of my generation
is that a
human being can
alter his life
by altering his
attitudes of mind."

WILLIAM JAMES (1842-1910)

Chapter One

History Of Change Technology

How does one approach the world with techniques so far divergent from main stream knowledge? Well the truth of the matter is that Neuro-Linguistic Programming, Imagery and Self-Talk are not really far removed modalities for change -- they have just been conveniently renamed to give the therapist or speaker the freedom to use the techniques.

The definitions for each of these modalities follows along the same presuppositions as will be found in this writing and supports the premise that if one person can master a skill or behavior, then it is possible to model that person and train another to learn and master that same skill or behavior.

I have spent quite some time now deliberating over how to present a clear dictionary-style definition of hypnosis. I have come to the conclusion that it is probably only definable through experience. Once defined, one might say it is very similar to the explication of visualization. This is because, in most cases, while utilizing the process of imagery, the person is in a state of hypnosis without knowing it at all. Andre M. Weitzenhoffer describes hypnosis as, *"a condition or state of selective hyper suggestibility brought about in an individual (subject) through the use of certain specific psychological or physical manipulations of this individual by another person (hypnotist)."* He goes on to state that *". . . self-hypnosis is equivalent to a two-person interaction in which part of the self appears to take over the role of hypnotist . . ."*[2] Therefore, the above definition would apply to self-hypnosis as well.

Although somewhat more vague than Weitzenhoffer's, my definition is as follows:

> *Hypnosis is a selected state of consciousness that*
> *one enters into for a specific purpose.*

---

[2]Weitzenhoffer, Andre' M., General Techniques of Hypnotism, 1957, Grune & Stratton, Inc. pg. 32

Less than vague you might say? Precisely my point. Hypnosis can be used for anything and everything relating to the mind. Although best known for habit and behavior changes, hypnosis has proven to be highly effective for life enhancement, study skills, relaxation and even increased intuition. It has improved and often saved marriages and is extremely effective for sexual dysfunction. The list is endless. The front cover of my center's information booklet says it best: *"All Positive Change Starts in the Mind."*[3] Can you think of a truer statement?

Let us begin at the beginning. Although I believe hypnosis and imagery have been used since the dawn of man, typically without conscious knowledge of what was at play, I will start with what little is known of its practice through history. Ages ago in the temples of Egypt the high priests and initiates would use forms of imagery and hypnosis to train the more affluent officials on how to overcome physical pain. The use of a mystical form of hypnosis was used to forecast future events as well. In another part of the world, ancient Greece, there were what was known as sleeping rooms. The priests of the time served the same function that a hypnotherapist performs in modern times. They would relax the person, usually a high official, and guide him through the past or into the future. The sleeping rooms were often used for visionary strategic planning and for contact with the gods.

Hypnosis has been given many different names over the centuries. Whether it was known as mesmerism, meditation, or hypnosis, the basis of its use was to go to that specific state and, most importantly, for a purpose. Hypnosis and imagery methods didn't start gaining any real notice until a flamboyant gentleman by the name of F. Anton Mesmer started his own brand of hypnotism over 200 years ago. His colorful ways brought attention to this unseen power that is within every one of us. The term *"mesmerized"* was coined after his processes became widely known. Mesmer was quite flashy and mystical in his work. Through the use of his eyes and a series of waves of the hands and arms he built an incredible intensity between himself and the subject. Although he didn't thoroughly understand it, Mesmer believed that this whole process was caused by some sort of magnetic effect. He asserted that the human body contained a certain fluid that accounted for the phenomena of magnetism and that this effect could emanate from the eyes and the hands of the *"magnetist" (himself)*. We know today that the effect was actually produced by something very different. He had only a small portion of the puzzle, but it

---

[3]Positive Changes, Inc. Copyright 1990

did lay the foundation for what is known today as hypnosis, visualization and imagery.

It was Dr. James Braid who coined the term Hypnosis, naming it after the Greek word *Hypno* meaning *sleep.* Since this identification it has possibly been the most widely misunderstood state in history. You see, in a state of hypnosis most people, even in the deepest trance, will remember what was said and experienced throughout the session. It is only a small cross section of the population that will awaken with amnesia after a session of hypnosis. Many people cannot tell the difference between a hypnotized state and a *"waking"* state, and will insist that hypnosis did not occur when it most definitely did. During a stage hypnosis performance a young man may be asked whether he believes he is hypnotized, and he will respond with a most emphatic "no!" But the hypnotist need only say the word "sleep" and he will immediately fall like a limp dishrag into a deep state. Upon awakening he will once again insist that he is not hypnotized, but will fall into an immediate hypnotic sleep with the suggestion to do so.

It is not the intention of this book to give you a historical breakdown on hypnosis, but to give you real proof that the client's knowledge that hypnosis occurred is not necessary for the change to be made. The purpose of this research is to give you a fresh look at what I have termed *Psycho-Linguistics "The Language of the Mind."* But like all types of therapy, there is a part to be played by the subject.

Although hypnosis and imagery, in one fashion or another, have always been used here on earth, some people still question its validity and usefulness. Let us take a moment to think of how we have come to be who we are right now. Our belief structure, whether valid or not, is what has molded us. It has in the past and will continue to be the role of others to shape our future unless we take back our power. This power is the power of choice. Hypnosis and/or imagery is by far the best modality for reaching that place where the belief structure was formed, and where it can be changed. I am referring to the unconscious mind.

It is true that a person in the state of hypnosis will not do anything that he or she would not agree to do otherwise. And, contrary to what you may have seen in the movies, a person is fully capable of dishonesty when under hypnosis. Naturally, hypnosis works best when there is a conscious desire on the part of the client to make the change. It is from this point that a well trained therapist will have the ability to access the client's bio-computer *(brain)* and feed in the appropriate suggestions. It is important to note that all of the participants in this research paid for the services that were rendered and therefore displayed the motivation needed for the therapy to work.

Mind technology, such as hypnosis, imagery and self-talk, is gaining more of a scientific basis all the time. In fact, with today's new technology, such as Neuro-Linguistic Programming, almost anyone can become a success at helping people as long as their heart and intentions are in the right place.

Also, the modern therapist will use scientific equipment such as advanced bio-feedback machines which utilize light and sound technology. These machines take care of placing the client into the receptive state needed for the new information to be accepted. In today's world it is becoming clear to people that the only thing limiting them is their own mind; or their ability to believe.

It is true in many respects that hypnosis is a conviction phenomenon. Indeed, the client must be convinced that the therapy will make a difference. Instilling this confidence is one of the most important jobs a counselor can perform. It is essential that the subject believe in a power greater than his or her own conscious mind for help and support. Once this belief system is instilled the therapist's job is well on its way. It is from here that the super-conscious can enter into the process and guide the client's thinking in the direction of the desired change.

When people become addicted, whether it is to drugs, food, alcohol or tobacco, they are, without exception, seeking a positive feeling. Therefore, all addictions have underlying positive intentions. Doug Rushkoff and Patrick Wells tell us that, *"Getting high is one of the most natural of human urges[4]."* All humans have a need for periods of non-ordinary consciousness and, because of this, it appears to be a biological urge. Unfortunately, during the drug war decade of the 90's, *"getting high"* is considered at worst illegal and at best irresponsible.

Through the use of *Psycho-Linguistics*, clients are taught that their positive intention, or high, is not only *"okay,"* it is necessary and natural. The individual is then guided to fill in the pieces for achieving a high without the need for any drugs or addictions. They can transform their addictive behavior into something positive and productive.

---

[4]Rushkoff, Douglas and Wells, Patrick, Free Rides -- How to Get High Without Drugs, 1991, Bantam Doubleday, Dell Publishing, New York, New York

It is a fact that everyone alive already knows how to get high naturally. Each person, as an infant, was an open channel to receive signals through all of the five senses. Because the newborn has no information upon which to judge the information received, everything is experienced and nothing is filtered. But, as the child grows into adulthood, he or she must put on filters as the ability to concentrate and learn becomes necessary. Soon the total aliveness of full-sensory experience is lost--but the memory of complete awareness remains.

Psycho-Linguistics is designed to darken, quiet and desensitize the remembrances of the less-than-positive experiences of the past and to re-awaken the memories of the natural joy found in living *"high."*

*"He who rejects change is the architect of decay.
The only human institution which rejects progress is the
cemetery."*

HAROLD WILSON

*"What you
get by
reaching your
destination
is not as
important as
what you
become by
reaching your
destination."*

DR. ROBERT ANTHONY

Chapter Two

What Is Hypnosis And Imagery?

My research displays strong evidence that there are innumerable misconceptions surrounding the science of hypnosis. Perhaps this relates to the beginnings of hypnosis, which were based in superstition and mysticism. The general public seems to maintain the belief that the hypnotist holds a special or mystical power, and indeed it would appear that way if you were watching a hypnotist perform a stage show. You cannot influence people to do something against their moral code or that they would not do with any other persuasion technique. The people who "perform" in a stage show must have agreed on some level to do what the hypnotist requests. The hypnosis process used in this research is termed "Ericksonian" after the renowned psychiatrist Dr. Milton Erickson. His processes involved creating a relaxed mind to aid in the treatment of mental disorders. Unlike the stage hypnotist who takes away conscious control, through the Ericksonian model control is given to the patient.

Hypnosis in this context is not brain washing but may be more appropriately termed brain cleansing. When an individual comes to a trained hypnotherapist, he or she is usually in a state of loss. For example, a woman who has smoked cigarettes for 35 years and is now in poor health probably holds the belief that she lacks "willpower" and is convinced that she can't make this change on her own. In other words she has hypnotized herself into believing that she can't change on her own. It is the hypnotist's assignment to cleanse her mind of such a limited thought and direct her back to the power within her.

You see, it is our natural and divine right to have whatever we want within our lives. One of my favorite lines from the Bible reads, "If you abide in me, and my words abide in you, ask whatever you wish, and it will be done for you."[5] There are no limitations within this statement. Thus, it applies in every area of your life.

---

[5]John 15:7 NASB

Another fallacy about hypnosis is that only weak-minded people can be hypnotized. This is totally false, and in fact, the reverse is true. The higher intelligence level of the client, the better hypnosis, imagery or any other change technology will work. After all, hypnosis is a tool. People don't really change because of hypnosis, but they do make changes while in a state of hypnosis. There is a subtle difference. In the state of hypnosis you are experiencing an expanded state of consciousness or awareness. It is a state where solutions are stored as possibilities. Here is where the therapist's role becomes vital. The job of the therapist is to help the subject access these solutions and apply them in his or her life. All hypnosis is self-hypnosis -- without the willingness of the subject the therapist's job is almost certain to fail.

With the techniques outlined in this book people will be able to guide themselves or others through the hypnotic process; from the first meeting, through the gathering of necessary information, to the layout of a successful plan of action, and client follow up. There are, however, a few steps that need to be taken before you even begin. The key to success in the therapy field is to be armed with a toolbox full of useful techniques and processes which will guide the client to success. First and foremost, you must be able to put yourself into the hypnotic state.

The TEN STEPS To SELF-HYPNOSIS:

In its true sense, all hypnosis is self-hypnosis. Only the person going into the hypnotic state, for whatever purpose, has the ability to make the change happen. Whether the participants are using these techniques or another, the hypnotic state is simply the method of access to the place within the mind where the new and more appropriate choices can be created.

There are numerous ways to put yourself into the altered state of hypnosis. From there it is up to you. Whether you are going into trance using a key word such as *"aum,"* or by rolling your eyes up to a ten o'clock position, you are practicing the science of hypnosis. Over the years it has been called many things; mind control, transcendental meditation (TM), or even prayer. All of these altered states fall under the definition of self-hypnosis and/or imagery. Remember the previous definition: Hypnosis is a selected state of consciousness that one enters into for a specific purpose.

This first technique of hypnosis is what I would consider one of the easiest and quickest for anyone to master. It is important to point out that deep altered states are not necessary for profound change to occur, but it does help the body to release some of the unconscious stress of the day thereby freeing up the energy of the mind to work on the specific solution at hand. The easiest way to use this outline is to read the directions into a tape recorder and then play it back one or two times a day or until the process is learned without the script.

Interestingly, there is a stage performer who goes by the name of *"The Amazing Kreskin,"* who says he is willing to pay $100,000 to anyone who can prove that the hypnotic state exists. His claim is that there is no such state as hypnosis, only the *"power of suggestion."* He uses this same technique in his seminars. Although he swears that this is not hypnosis, it just further proves the overall ignorance about hypnosis and the level of misinformation still being presented to the community.

1.   **Get into a comfortable position.** *You will soon discover that relaxation is a key element to the hypnotic state.   Place yourself in a comfortable chair or lie down. Choose another location besides your bed since this is your place of sleep. For this procedure to be effective you will want to remain completely aware. Place your hands comfortably by your side or in your lap. From this moment on concentrate on your breathing. Begin to connect the breath as you breathe in and out. In time this will come natural to you and conscious effort will no longer be necessary. Breathe in a full breath and at the end release a full breath and then repeat the process. This alone is capable of putting you into an altered state of consciousness.*

2.   **Close your eyes and repeat three times to yourself the amount of time you wish to remain in the hypnotized state.** *You will find that in the state of self-hypnosis there is no time, or more precisely, while in a deep state you are unaware of time. There is a scientific explanation for this phenomenon. Without getting too complicated at this point, let me explain. We all operate within four basic brain wave patterns. They are known as Beta, which is wide awake; Alpha, which is a relaxed state and has also been found through research to be a powerful learning state; Theta, also a very relaxed state and a place for super learning; and; Delta, associated with deep sleep. Hypnosis, and a state of super-learning, occur within the brain wave states of Alpha and Theta. While a subject is in these states there appears to be a sense of time distortion; one minute could feel like an hour. Within these states and what occurs there, time does not seem to exist or have any impact on the subject, and access to a greater reality is then granted. In actuality, that reality is your full imagination, which is the true tool of hypnosis or any change technology.*

Also, the state may feel so good to you that without giving yourself the suggestion to return within a particular time frame, you could find yourself staying in the self-hypnotic state for hours at a time. Although this would not bring about any problem, it is not necessary. Hypnosis is known for fast and effective change and there really isn't any reason to stay in hypnosis for more than 20 to 30 minutes at a time.

3.   Imagine a blackboard and place the number 25 on it. *Envision yourself erasing that number and it being replaced by the number 24. Each number is guiding you deeper than the number before. Continue this process until you reach zero. This process gives your conscious mind something to do while your unconscious mind relaxes your body.*

4.   Become aware of your body and scan it for the level of relaxation achieved. *Imagine that you are filling your body up with a solution that will protect and keep you from harm. The purpose of this is to narrow your attention down to the different parts of your body and give you the feeling of being in a safe place. It is from this safe place that your unconscious mind will successfully help you through the changes.*

5.   Imagine that you are creating your ideal place of relaxation. *Create a place where you can be comfortable and at peace. This ideal place of relaxation could be anywhere or at any time. Whether on a sandy beach with the ocean waves lapping at your feet, or atop a mountain with a clean, brisk breeze ruffling your hair and cooling your cheeks, it is your creation. There are no limits here. Each time that you go to your ideal place you can make enhancements so inventing it will be enjoyable every time.*

6.   Go now to that personal place of relaxation and imagine yourself drifting off into a dream, and in the dream all that you want, all that you need and all that you desire has come true. *(Remember, in dreams all things are possible and there are no limitations to consciousness.) This step is important in the process of self-imagery because dreams are a surefire way of making contact with the unconscious mind, which is the part of you that will create successful changes in the future.*

7.   Step into your dream. *Begin to see what you would be seeing, hear what you would be hearing and feel what you would be feeling. Act as if everything is actually happening all around you. Every night during* *our dreams we are given suggestions by the unconscious mind. Yet we often neglect to listen to our nighttime counsel, discounting the information as "just a dream." But remember that your mind is a servo-mechanism--a goal striving, success oriented, bio-chemical machine that doesn't know how to fail. However, problems arise if we have fed in failure information. The bio-computer cannot help but feed the same failure information back. When this happens, it is time to make a change; and that is what imagery is all about. Everyone is working perfectly. People are not wrong or broken; they have just been misinformed. They tend to believe that if they continue to think and act in the same way that somehow, some way, a different outcome is just around the corner. But, as the saying goes, if you continue to think what you have always thought, you will continue to get what you have always got! So be brave and live your dreams.*

8.   Move yourself into the future to the date and time when you are convinced that you have and deserve your wants, needs and desires. (You are creating a vacuum for your mind where it can place your wishes into sequence.) *The relevance of this step is two-fold. First, hypnosis and/or imagery is a conviction phenomenon in more ways than one. You must be convinced that you can and will have your wants, needs and desires fulfilled. Secondly, in order for hypnosis to work you must place into sequence the successful steps that your bio-computer will need to follow.*[6]

9.   Starting from that future date and moving backwards in time make a review in your mind of all that you will do and all that you will experience to bring about the fulfillment of your desires. The purpose of this step is to give your bio-computer an alternate view of the future by storing it as if the success has already occurred.

10.   Count yourself back to fully awakened consciousness. *Give yourself the following suggestion: "I'm going to count from one to five and at the count of five I will be wide awake, feeling fine and in perfect health. One . . . Two . . . Three . . . All changes and modifications are being made from my superconscious to my conscious mind . . . Four . . . and, Five . . . wide awake." Take three full breaths realizing with each breath that all you have*

---

[6]Ask, and it shall be given to you; seek, and you shall find; knock, and it shall be opened to you. Matthew 7:7 NASB

experienced is now truth for you . . . and this is so. Understand that you are bringing yourself from a state near sleep to wide awake in a matter of seconds. Some people seem to maintain the misinformation that it is possible to be stuck in hypnosis forever. This is totally false. It is impossible for someone to remain in the state permanently, and this has never happened. You would simply fall into a natural sleep and awaken after a short nap.

Who Can Be Hypnotized?

Generally speaking, every normal person is hypnotizable -- that is, people with an I.Q. of at least 70 who have no severe mental disorders. It is my personal opinion that even those with IQs below 70 could be helped by the right therapist. Throughout my fifteen years around the different mind technologies, I have been witness to many fantastic transformations for a variety of people from all walks of life. It has been proven to me time and again that there are truly no limits to consciousness or the mind's ability to make behavior changes and enhancements.

It is here that I would like to outline a few techniques which helped us to choose those clients who would have the ability to reach a deep hypnotic state. Remember that deep trance states are not a prerequisite to change, but rather a resource.

The following tests are given to help in assessing what percentage will accept direct suggestions and what percentage will need inferred suggestions. Some people will, by nature, accept what you are saying and go along with all that you ask of them (direct). Others will assume or infer that they know what you "mean" for them to do (inferred). This will be explained in more detail as we move through the techniques.

"Success is not the result of spontaneous combustion.
You must set yourself on fire."
REGGIE LEACH

Testing Processes:

For simplicity in writing, this portion will assume that we are testing a male client, although the techniques will work with equal effect for both men and women.

A.   FINGER MAGNETS. Have the subject place his hands together separating the two index fingers. Ask him to look down at his fingers and imagine that at the fingertips there are two magnets and they are being drawn together. Once the fingers touch together give strong suggestions that he will not be able to take them apart. In fact, the harder he tries the more difficult it will become. Once these suggestions are given, ask him to *"try to take them apart."* Watch his attempts and when he has failed a few times give him the suggestion that at the count of three his fingers will easily come apart.

Don't become concerned with whether the subject is able to take his fingers apart. Rather, look for his ability to accept a direct suggestion. The purpose of the test is to find those subjects who can create what is known as selective thinking and also to screen those subjects who test as inferred suggestible. In truth, you are testing your subject's imagination and ability to take a direct suggestion. Some people will become concerned when they suspect that they have failed a test. They begin to fear that they are not hypnotizable. It is virtually impossible to fail the test. Under no circumstances do you tell your clients that they have failed a test. Simply explain that they are going through a testing process which they cannot fail. These tests are for you, the hypnotist, to gather information that you will use later during the altered state.

What these processes uncovered was a strong correlation between "Right Brain Thinkers" being more directly suggestible and "Left Brain Thinkers" more inferred. This result is logical since the right hemisphere controls creativity and the left hemisphere controls precise thinking. In reality the test result is of little importance to the subject but is of immeasurable value to a trained therapist who will utilize the information later during the altered state.

When testing subjects who are inferred, it is very important that you point out to them that hypnosis or change cannot occur without their consent. I let them know that they were being tested on their imagination, not intelligence. It is essential for an inferred subject to know that there is no failure; only feedback. So keep your perceptual filters open for any clues that your subject might display.   The above statement is true for all testing processes.

B.   HAND CLASP.   Place the subject's hands straight out in front of him in a clasp and have him imagine that as he squeezes down a vise is pressing against the outside of the hands making it impossible for him to separate them.   Give the suggestion that as he tries to take his hands apart it will become more and more difficult.   Then, ask him to *"just try to take them apart."*   Watch the hands closely.   Then tell him that at the count of three the vise will be released and his hands will be free.   Count him out by counting from one to three to ensure a return to full awareness.

C.   BALLOON & BOOK.   The subject places his hands straight out in front of his body.   Have him imagine that a balloon has been tied to the wrist of one hand.   Ask him to turn the other hand over and imagine that a heavy book has been placed in it and as the book is getting heavier and heavier the other hand is becoming lighter and lighter, as if the balloon is lifting it into the air.   Ask him to close his eyes and use his imagination.   When there is a distance between the two hands, have him open his eyes and look at the placement of his hands.   If your subject's hands did not move, which will be the case if the subject is inferred, simply ask him to return his hands to his lap only as slowly as he can recognize the difference between the two.   When his hands return to his lap, ask him to open his eyes once again.

D.   EYE ROLL TEST.   Place your finger on the forehead at the hairline of the subject and ask him to keep his eyes open and roll them upward as if looking through the top of his head at the place where your finger is touching.   Give him the suggestion that with his eyes rolled upward to slowly close the eyelids down.
Pay attention to the amount of white of the eye that is showing as the eyelids roll down.   If there is a good portion of white showing and only a small amount of the iris visible, chances are that the subject is a deep subject.   No one quite knows what the connection is or why this phenomena occurs, but it has proven true time and again.

E.   EYE CLOSURE.   This technique can be used immediately following the Eye Roll Test or alone.   Ask the subject to close his eyes and imagine that the eyelids are so loose, so limp, and so relaxed that he won't be able to open them.   *(Compound the suggestion).*   When you feel that he is relaxed, suggest *"just try to open them."* Watch closely as he tries, and when he has failed a few times, give him the suggestion that at the count of three his eyes will open and he will once again be wide awake. Count him back up from one to three.

F. HYPNOTIC STARE. The Hypnotic Stare is the process most commonly associated with stage hypnosis and should be used with extreme caution. I use this test only with those subjects who have previously tested as deep subjects.

Ask the subject to look into your eyes and not to look away. *(You will continuously gaze directly at the point between the eyes at the bridge of his nose, and not look away.)* Place your hands at the sides of the subject's head a few inches away to block peripheral vision. Give the suggestion, *"You are going to listen to my voice and my voice only . . . Your eyelids are getting heavier and heavier but you are going to try to keep them open . . . heavier and heavier."* Continue with the suggestions until the eyelids flutter and then give the command, *"Sleep!"* **Be prepared to catch the subject.**

The purpose in these tests is actually two-fold. First, they let you know just how willingly the person's conscious mind will take part in the session. For one reason or another the young man in this example has sought out a therapist for assistance. Before you would be able to effectively help him make his desired changes, his modes of access and communication must be discovered. These tests let you determine how his bio-computer takes in information. If his bio-computer takes his hands apart during the Finger Magnets or Hand Clasp technique, you know that his mind is taking suggestions in an inferred way. Because he is inferring your meaning, You, as the therapist, will need to use inferred language patterns. The best way to access an inferred subject is through sleight-of-mouth patterns. Also known as imbedded commands, sleight-of-mouth patterns are used to persuade someone to do something without specifically telling him or her what to do.

If during the Finger Magnet technique the test subject's fingers stuck together or during the Hand Clasp test the hands remained clasped tightly, then there is a strong possibility that he will respond well to direct suggestion. A subject that is directly suggestible will most likely be more responsive, or able to do suggested movements with his physical body. This in no way means that the person who doesn't pass these tests successfully is unable to use hypnosis. Rather, what this has proven is that as long as the right patterns were given and the inferred person was allowed to place them into his or her own context, the results were the same. The purpose is not only to find out whether he can successfully imagine, but it also lets you know if he takes direct suggestion or if he is making inferences in his mind as to what you are suggesting or want him to do.

The same is true with the Balloon and Book technique except it allows the therapist to more fully access the client's imagination. If you find that his imagination process is very good, even if he failed the two tests previous to the Balloon test, you will find that he is a very good subject for hypnosis. Remember, it is the job of the hypnotherapist to cultivate the imagination. Because the imagination is such a powerful state of consciousness, it is probably the most important access. In truth, hypnosis or imagery is the use of the mind, or the use of the imagination, to accomplish a goal.

The Eye Roll and Eye Closure tests are used every day in our center. These tests will help the subject to create a selective state of consciousness. In that state the person can receive a direct suggestion to follow and this is the therapist's opportunity to discover whether he is going to go along with the suggestions. From the Eye Roll and Eye Closure the subject can be taken directly from testing into a deep state of relaxation. The deeper the individual can go into relaxation, the better he will respond upon awakening. This is because the brain wave patterns can be influenced by deep relaxation. In hypnotherapy you are accessing the brain wave patterns of Alpha and Theta. With most subjects in a clinical setting you will be accessing in the realm of Alpha.

"True silence is the rest of the mind;
it is to the body, nourishment and refreshment.

WILLIAM PENN

Direct vs. Inferred Suggestibility

It is unfortunate that most hypnotherapists are taught only a directly suggestible approach. They are trained to place someone into a trance, tell him or her exactly what to see, hear and experience and then expect everyone placed under their spell to go out and make changes exactly as directed. Stage hypnosis has proven that only one out of every ten people is truly directly suggestible. These are the people who can be told that ammonia is perfume and, while inhaling it deeply, smell a sweet and flowery scent. With these clients you are able to perform physical manifestations, such as hand levitation, to demonstrate the direct phenomena of a hypnotic state. These people usually will be aware that they have been in an altered state and will experience a much deeper trance than most.

On another end of the spectrum we have the inferred suggestible person or, as known by some hypnotherapists, the emotionally suggestible subject. It is not very likely that a standard direct suggestion will have any effect over an inferred client. However, if you imply suggestions toward a planned direction, the inferred client can then create the change.

As an example, *"I'm not sure exactly when these changes are going to take place, but you are."* This suggestion offers an outlet for the imagination to take over and place the changes where your client wants them.

To an inferred suggestible person the following direct suggestion would probably not be effective: *"You are going to change your smoking habits for good. Upon awakening you will crush your pack of cigarettes and be a non-smoker forever."*

This is a very direct suggestion. The inferred suggestible client's mind would probably be very busy trying to figure out how and when this may or may not occur. And, if this client didn't immediately arise from the session with an urge to crush a pack of cigarettes he or she would be quite convinced that the therapy did not work. To an inferred suggestible person you would be more likely to set up success with:

"I'm not sure what happened during this time of relaxation, but you are. Something wonderful happened and upon awakening you will find the right time, and I'm not sure exactly what time that will be, but you will rid yourself completely of tobacco and nicotine without any conscious effort. You will simply walk away. It could be today upon awakening, it could be tomorrow, or in weeks to come, but at some time you will make the decision to deal with the problem once and for all -- to set yourself free. That's right, it may be as early as today."

When dealing with an inferred suggestible person, it's important that he or she is always being guided in the direction of an outcome. This is where the suggestibility testing comes into play. If someone is unable to do the testing, such as when the direct suggestion is given that the eyelids and muscles are so loose, limp and relaxed that they won't open at all and then the eyes pop open, there is a pretty good chance that this person is an inferred suggestible person. What was heard in his or her mind was *"You can't open your eyes,"* and the immediate response was *"Yes, I can,"* and the eyes flew open. The directly suggestible person would create the response by simply imagining the eyelids heavy and relaxed. The direct person's response would be, *"Okay, I can imagine that,"* and the eyes will remain locked into place.

Another quick and easy tip is to monitor the way in which people present information. If they infer information while communicating to others, their brain will usually take in directly suggestible comments. If they communicate directly, then there is a strong probability that they will take inferred suggestions inwardly. There is a phenomena within the brain that will cause it to do the opposite when giving out information from the way in which it is received.

Imagination

The imagination is perhaps the most vital ingredient to the *Psycho-Linguistic* session as well as any therapeutic session. The word imagination is, in my opinion, misspelled; it should be spelled *image-a-nation*. A *nation* represents a person's map of reality *(the belief structure),* and *image*, means the way that map is perceived within the individual's mind.

If, in your imagination, you can paint a picture, and can hear the sounds and experience the feelings, then you have imaged it and now it is a nation (map of reality) in your mind. What you are perceiving in your mind will come to pass as reality. The bio-computer, or the brain, now has all necessary information for bringing this new reality into being through behaviors, attitudes and actions.

Brain Wave Patterns

We all have a balance of brain waves at play during our day, whether during activity, while sedentary, or even in deep sleep. Our brain's rhythms move from Beta to Alpha, through Theta and into Delta off and on throughout the day. It is through these brain waves that we access the memories or sequences of thought which make up our personalities and create the differences between us. It has been proven time and again, by many successful therapists, that when a subject is in a relaxed and receptive state he or she is in the best position for making a behavior change that will be permanent.

Many of our history's most successful inventors, such as Albert Einstein, functioned in the Alpha brain wave pattern far more often than in the

Beta realm. In the Alpha and Theta brain wave rhythms there is a noticeable release of stress, strain and frustration. You will want to inform your clients that they are, indeed, going into a specific state which is perhaps a bit out of phase from the conscious everyday Beta--wide awake--state.

Although there are four distinctive brain wave patterns, every human brain functions in multiple brain wave activity.

1.   Beta State. *(20-13 cycles per second)* Beta is the state in which your conscious mind is accessed. It is the wide awake state in which you keep track of your life, such as paying your bills, setting up your appointment calendar for the day, and balancing your checkbook. It is your analytical mind. Within its realm is the part of you that is at times self-conscious and at other times controlling. This is the awakened state of consciousness and within this realm fear, frustration, anxiety and self-doubt reside.

2.   Alpha State. *(13 to 7 cycles per second)* When you are feeling very creative, relaxed and at ease, you are probably functioning in alpha. This is the place where there is no time and no limitations. In Alpha your creative juices seem to flow without end and the body is in a place of serenity. If you have ever watched an artist at work, you will notice how creativity can seem to emanate from within the physical body. The artist's eyes are usually very intense, but other-worldly, and the body seems to flow as if each limb were poured from a rich fluid. If tested, the artist's brain wave pattern would surely be within the ranges of Alpha. Most artists, writers, composers, and poets can work for long hours, often through the night, without any awareness of the time as it ticks away on the clock and then will suddenly be amazed when realizing the amount of time that has elapsed. Alpha knows no time and holds no limitations. One easy way to reach the pleasant state of Alpha is by quietly listening to Baroque music.

3.   Theta State. *(7 to 4 cycles per second)* Meditation is the best known access to the Theta state of consciousness. It is a deeply relaxed state on the brink of sleep. With the help of certain machines such as light and sound devices or through training processes the Theta state can be attained. Most people are unable to do this consciously. Because it exists on the fine line of sleep, it is difficult to maintain the state without falling into sleep.

4.   Delta State. *(4 to 0 cycles per second)* Once the brain wave pattern of delta is reached, the subject is asleep. This is the place of dreams and visions that no one has quite been able to define. Delta is not generally used in hypnosis, but it is possible to communicate with a sleeping person using hypnotic techniques.

At times a subject will appear to move from a state of deep relaxation into sleep and then awaken later. It should be noted here that there has never been a case where someone was placed in the hypnotic state and then was unable to return. He or she would simply fall into a natural sleep and would soon awaken normally as if having received a deep, relaxing sleep.

Testing your subjects will give you the information necessary for a successful hypnotic session. Remember, hypnosis is a selective mind state. You are now ready to get the feel for placing yourself or another into that state. The following dialogue is designed for you to either read to someone or to speak into a tape recorder.

You will want to become aware of your voice at this point. Listen closely to the tone and cadence of your voice so that you begin to include the hypnotic tone and tempo which is a part of the hypnotic session. It takes practice, but as you use your voice you will begin to articulate in a smooth and comfortable way so that others will be able to follow along and be soothed by its sound. Recording these dialogues on tape and then playing them back to yourself is an excellent way to monitor your voice and your articulation.

BRAINWAVE FREQUENCIES

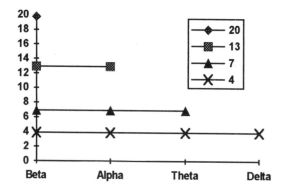

Induction Technique:

Begin by directing yourself or your subject to look at a specific spot on the ceiling or a wall.[7]

DIALOGUE

Take a moment and become aware of a spot, any spot at all, and notice the lightness and darkness of that spot . . . and, as you do this, your eyelids are getting heavier and heavier but I want you to keep them open . . . keep them open for as long as you can.

As you continue to look at that spot try to keep your eyes open finding that the harder you try the more difficult it becomes.

Place into that spot the ideal you with all skills and all abilities. Soon, and very soon indeed you will find your eyes closing. As your eyes close now you will find yourself drifting into a dreamy-drowsy feeling of sleep. Just let your eyes close now . . . comfortably and relaxed . . . just letting go . . . letting go of all thoughts, all cares, all anxieties of the day.

From here become aware of your body . . . and as you do allow each and every part of your body to go loose, limp and completely relaxed. In fact, you are going so relaxed . . . so completely relaxed that the seconds are like hours, the hours are like days and the days become weeks. Allow yourself this time to relax, releasing all conscious thoughts and cares of the day to drift away. Allow the feelings of peace, tranquillity and spaciousness to enter into your mind.

From your mind move into your imagination where you can begin to build a place around you . . . a place where you can drift away on a personal vacation . . . a vacation that will allow you to return with a fresh attitude about life and about your world . . . a healthy new attitude that will bring you more of what you want . . just when you want it the most. In a moment my voice will

---

[7]The purpose of having the subject focus on one particular spot is to create selective thinking. This is what is needed to get the subject to concentrate on your voice and allow the thoughts of the day to drift away.

pause and when it does you will find the seconds will become hours and the hours will become days. At that time you will project your mind into this vacation place. When my voice returns it will not startle you at all. In fact, it will place you into a deeper and more relaxed place in consciousness . . . It will be from that place that your new attitude will begin to grow and prosper becoming reality for you upon awakening . . . and this is so . . . (pause)

Now as you relax and slowly return to this room, you will find that you can return only as slowly as you can incorporate the new attitude into your life . . . your world . . . and your experience. I will now count from one to five and at the count of five your eyes will open, you will feel wide awake and in perfect health . . . natural and normal in every way . . 1 . . 2 . . 3 . . 4 . . . 5. Eyes open, wide awake and in perfect health . . . and this is so.

"Peace is rarely denied to the peaceful."

JOHANN VON SCHILLER

Chapter Three

Neuro-Linguistic Programming

You will soon discover the connection between Neuro-Linguistic Programming (**NLP**) and hypnosis, self-talk, and imagery, as it relates to the use of Psycho-Linguistics in helping yourself or other people to attain desired outcomes.

"Self-Talk" is the newest fad in self-help and is probably the fastest growing method of change technology. It involves a variety or combination of methods from spoken affirmations to scripting and dialoging. Self-talk is directed at accessing the old tape programs that were established throughout childhood and replacing them with new, more appropriate messages that will better serve the individual. Self-talk is also an extension of NLP which will be discussed more specifically during the section about auditory changes in therapy.

It is my belief that the terms *"imagery," "visualization"* and *"hypnosis"* are often misused. By this I mean to say that in truth all states are in essence the same, and for our purpose here these terms will be used interchangeably. NLP has taken imagery methods to the next level of understanding, and the founders of NLP have done a fine job of outlining the visualization process as the principal component of sub-modality work *(defined later in this chapter)*. In the section defining visual processing, I will cover the usage of imagery more thoroughly.

As Richard Bandler has said, *"Everything is hypnosis or nothing is hypnosis."* Even though many people have tried to call the processes by different names *(visualization, imagery, self-talk, affirmations)* it really boils down to the same basic ingredients--the ones found in hypnosis. It is like the old adage, *by any other name, a rose is still a rose.*

Prayer is another method that seems to have been left out from most therapy programs whether it is private counseling, books or seminars. I feel that this is mostly because of the wide variance in religious preferences. When you begin discussing the way in which someone prays, you are touching into some very sensitive material. During my work I recommend that those individuals who have a specific religious belief pray along the guidelines of their faith. Those who have no religious beliefs are asked to consider the possibility that something greater than themselves is at work in the universe. We have adopted the philosophy of Alcoholics Anonymous--an individual person in and of his or her self probably cannot change, but with the help of this universal power all things are possible.

What is NLP? (Neuro-Linguistic Programming)

Perhaps it is best to explain what NLP is by relating just how it all came about. The founders of the process that is today known as NLP, Richard Bandler and John Grinder, made a nearly life-long study of successful therapists, their techniques and methods of communication with clients, and just what brought about consistently positive outcomes. Out of that quest the patterns of NLP evolved. These patterns are rooted in linguistics and non-verbal communication and are structured so that anyone with a desire to help themselves or others can follow the guidelines to achieve a similar level of success.

It is not the purpose of this book to fully define or teach you NLP. There is an abundance of books available that cover the theory and principles quite effectively. It is my intention to show you, in text format, how I have taken what I learned in my training with some of the masters of NLP, combined it with the processes of hypnosis, imagery and mind control, and converted it into a successful practice of helping people to achieve their outcomes.

For our context of therapy there was one flaw with the NLP techniques as they stood alone. Within the NLP structure the founders created their own language; a terminology they decided was best suited for their method of teaching the techniques to others. We found that these language patterns became awkward outside the structure of the NLP world. Since most people seeking therapy have no knowledge of NLP, we found it necessary to adapt the language to fit their needs. With *Psycho-Linguistics* I have given the patterns of NLP a degree of usefulness for the layman.

You will find a list of excellent books on NLP listed in the back of the text. These books are not required reading for Psycho-Linguistics to work for you; they are simply well-written books that will help you to expand your knowledge if that is what you desire. If you would like to know more about NLP after reading *Psycho-Linguistics*, please note the books that are listed in the bibliography.

Major Presuppositions Of NLP

Although there will be exceptions to all of these presuppositions, they are a very useful starting place for communication. After incorporating the NLP guidelines into my private therapy, I found my modest practice flourishing into a thriving business, with a referral rate that more than tripled and with offices in three cities.

1.   Communication is redundant.   People are always communicating in all three major representational systems *(Visual, Auditory, and Kinesthetic/feelings)*. When you can figure out through which system an individual is accessing, you can present your information through that same channel and in a way so that he or she can then make the decision to use it.

2.   The meaning of your communication is the response that you elicit. Communication is not about what you intend to relay, nor is it about saying the right words. Rather, it is about creating an experience and eliciting a response from the listener. The bottom line is the response you invoke. In any therapy you must first know where you are going so that you know when you get there. NLP gives clearly defined outcomes that lead one to a successful process in therapy or communication.

3.   People respond to their perception of reality, not to reality itself. NLP is the science of changing perception -- not reality. It seems that when the perceptions are changed, reality will follow suit; that is, when that which is changed is also that which is most constant. I have a favorite saying I use with clients in the state of hypnosis, *"If you want a constant change, change what is most constant -- You."*

4.   People work perfectly.   No one is wrong or broken; it is simply a matter of finding out how that person functions now so that you can effectively change to something more desirable. This is perhaps one of NLP's greatest discoveries. This one small statement has almost completely lifted the burden of explanation, of endlessly illustrating to clients why certain processes work. Over 70% of the clients we see each day at our centers come to us to stop smoking. I tell these people that they have trained themselves to smoke so well that they now need my help to get them to stop. This typically brings a surprised look, but it is a truth with which they usually can relate. I then give them the spark of possibility, *"What if that part of you, the one that trained you so well to be a smoker, could be retrained to do something useful and beneficial?"* This idea is usually gladly accepted. Remember it is not bad to have an addictive personality so long as you are addicted to good things, such as exercising, eating healthy foods and enjoying life.

5.　**People always make the best choice available to them at the time, although there are often better choices.** How many times have you said to yourself, *"If only I could go back in time and change my decision"?* Wouldn't it be great if you could bring the awareness of the future back with you to the present? Although this is not, technically, what occurs in hypnosis and NLP, it is, in a way, true. You are going ahead in time through the use of your imagination. The future that you perceive is then stored as your past, and you almost automatically begin to make choices with the new, updated information.

6.　**Every behavior is useful in some context.** In the world of NLP, this is a simple step called reframing: to find out where and when a given behavior is useful, even if it is not necessarily positive. At times you really have to stretch it, but when you begin to look at a problem as an asset, something shifts in the mind, and it seems to lose its unconscious power over you. You are then free to make new choices that are just as immediate and hopefully more appropriate.

7.　**Choice is always better than no choice.** Have you ever noticed how wild animals react when they are trapped in a corner with no place to turn? Isn't that just the way we act when mental or physical stress has got us trapped, as if there is no way out when, in fact, there could be many ways out of our dilemma? At times just becoming aware of the obvious choices might be all a person needs to successfully change a behavior that might have been with him or her since early childhood.

8.　**Anyone can do anything.** If one person can do something it is possible to model it and teach it to anyone else. In the circles of NLP these are known as submodalities. It is the study of the internal states of consciousness and how to make changes within them to support the outcome that is desired.

9. **People already have all the resources they need.** The only thing that may be lacking is the access to these resources at appropriate times and places. NLP gives the therapist skills not only for asking the right questions, but also for noticing the reactions so that when the appropriate response has been elicited, you can move on to making it a permanent and positive part of the person's life.

10. **There is no such thing as failure, only feedback.** Every response can be utilized. This was the motivation that started my research into which aspects of NLP, hypnosis or any other change technology would actually work in a private one-on-one situation. Surprisingly, I found that the methods didn't have to work perfectly for me to use them. I could pick and choose, combine and modify from them all, discovering which worked best for each personality.

11. **Anything can be accomplished by anyone if the task is broken down into small enough chunks.** Quite appropriately, this is termed *chunking.* Most people tend to do either all or nothing. Unfortunately, far too many choose to do nothing. It is with this in mind that I often use the statement, *"A little bit of something is certainly better than a whole lot of nothing."*

Establishing Rapport

Probably the first benefit that I received from NLP came in the discovery of rapport techniques which put me in control of the communication almost immediately. Sure, hypnotherapy talks about rapport and so does psychology, but NLP takes it one step further. You don't have to wait for rapport to develop, you can plan for and produce rapport through a series of successful processes that I will outline for you here.

DEFINITION: **Rapport** -- *to be in agreement or alignment with another; meeting a person on their own level by using familiar words and matching body language; verbal and nonverbal matching.*

Have you ever met someone and felt an instant kinship with that person? The two of you just seemed to click and the communication flowed easily and naturally. Perhaps it even felt as if you could spend hours just talking with this person, as if you had known him or her all of your life.

On the other hand, have you ever met a person with whom you could never quite get on the same wave-length? Communication may have been stilted with long silences and sentences started but not finished. This may have even evolved into feelings of frustration or dislike for this individual.

These types of communication are each end of the spectrum, and you will most likely encounter every type in-between. But what if you could have taken control of the communication with the "difficult" person? What if you knew how to get on that person's *"wave-length"*? Most likely the conversation would have ended with a totally different outcome -- the outcome you wanted!

All communication and change accomplished through Neuro-Linguistic Programming is through rapport, either on a conscious or unconscious level. There are several different styles for building and maintaining rapport. Admittedly, it is best to learn these techniques through hands-on seminar training; however, I will do my best to outline them in the text so that you can understand their importance and begin to benefit from their use.

Physical Matching:

In watching the most successful communicators, negotiators and mediators, you will see something special about their body posture. One of their hidden secrets to open communication is the matching of body language.

For the most effective communication choose to stand or sit in the same position as the person with whom you are talking. For example, if that person is sitting back with legs crossed and arms folded you will sit in an identical position. Psychologists use this tool to make their patients more comfortable about opening up to them. Use this technique in all your communications -- you will be quite amazed with the results.

You need not be concerned that the person will notice you mimicking their stance. Only at the unconscious level will he or she notice your imitations and this will be as a mirror image. This person is comfortable with his or her own self image and, since you look the same in your body position, you become non-threatening. The person becomes comfortable with you and begins to relax -- the barriers come down and the communication begins to flow.

You can learn to take the physical matching to the degree of the most effective communicators by studying and matching through practice and repetition, starting out consciously and then letting it flow to the unconscious level.

I once had a client who is an excellent example for the applications of matching and mirroring. "Scott" was never completely aware of the world around him, and to many he seemed rather obnoxious. He is what is known in the world of NLP as an *internal processor*, which means he thought that everything going on in his inner mind was what was actually occurring in the outer world. Therefore, he was unaware of other people's basic needs and his own, often inappropriate, communication. Scott is a highly intelligent fellow, but he had a limited ability for communicating his knowledge to others.

If you watched Scott from a distance, however, you could tell there were many things he could do differently to perhaps gain rapport with those to whom he was attempting to communicate. He seemed to have an inborn ability of breaking rapport instead of gaining or maintaining it. One day he came to the office, quite anxious and upset, and asked me if I could help him in acquiring a new job. His hope was that, through hypnosis, I could help him gain his self-confidence, self-esteem, self-worth and so on. But what I found out was that, more than anything else, Scott needed some essential conscious skills -- basic rapport skills. These are the skills that would allow him to make in-roads into the interviewer's unconscious awareness. Of course, people in a position of hiring will employ someone who is similar to them or meets the criteria of their needs.

I started by testing Scott and we found that he was a very good hypnotic subject. He was able to take suggestions and utilize them immediately. During his visits, we took him through role rehearsals and practiced the interview. Through a guided process of imagery I gave him the post-hypnotic suggestion that when he went into an interview he would put himself into *"state,"* which meant that he would begin to think of himself as successful, with the ability to speak and react appropriately. I worked with his unconscious mind and made an agreement that during an interview process he would match the tone and tempo of the interviewer's voice, match the breathing sequence of the interviewer and also match the physical body posture.

This would all be done without Scott's conscious mind knowing it. It was certainly okay if Scott wanted to do it consciously as well, but it was all set up on an unconscious level so that it would be relaxing to him and appear as a natural model, outside conscious awareness of the interviewer.

Scott came directly to my office from the interview more excited than I had ever seen him. He got the job. For the first time in his life, Scott had actually enjoyed the experience of a job interview. He said that the employer had actually sat and chatted with him for some time after they had discussed the position and then decided upon Scott for the position right then.

Unfortunately, less than a week after his successful interview I found Scott back in my office, this time looking more unhappy than ever before. *"What happened?"* I asked.

" I was fired," was his sullen reply.

Once Scott had landed the job he neglected to practice the techniques and repeat them on the job and in his everyday life. The interviewer liked him and found a comfortable rapport there. He felt that this was a person who could learn and do the job efficiently. But when Scott got into a situation with his immediate supervisor, he reverted to the old behaviors.

Scott needed to work on learning and practicing these skills on a conscious level as well as the unconscious. NLP is best known for conscious improvement that can have an immediate impact. These are the same conscious level skills best utilized by sales people; the non-verbal communication skills of matching, mirroring and rapport that allow you to pace and lead someone to the sale.

In truth, are we not selling ourselves every day, all day long? Doesn't it make sense that the more skills, abilities, and resources you have available to you to gain and maintain rapport and to lead someone where you want them to go, the more successful you will be in the world in general?

DEFINITIONS:

Matching -- Feeding back what you see as the external state of another.

Mirroring -- Feeding back in mirror image (opposite) what you see as the external state of another person.

Cross Over Mirroring -- Using one aspect of your behavior to match a different aspect of the other person's behavior. Examples: Adjust your voice to match the rhythm of the other person's breathing; pace their eye blinks with your finger movements; pace their voice tempo with the nodding of your head.

Types Of Physical Matching

A. **Body posture (whole, half, part body matching)** - *Sitting or standing - Body angle, stance; Position of arms, hands, legs and feet; Position of head and shoulder angles.*

B. **Gestures** - *Hand movements; Arm movements; Head movements; Body movements such as shrugs, body shifting, or head nodding*

C. **Breathing** - *Fast or slow; Upper, middle or lower chest; Through the nose or mouth*

D. **Voice** - *Tempo - fast or slow; Tonality - high or low; Timbre - deep or high; Intensity - excited or relaxed; Volume - loud, medium or soft*

E. **Facial expressions** - *Facial Appearance: eye blinks, smile, mouth opened or closed, scowl or frown, puckered lips, wrinkled nose, raised eyebrows*

One excellent method of practicing rapport skills, and matching in particular, is to begin to notice the actions of the people around you. Restaurants or social settings are the most opportune places to observe specific body cues of the people around you. Practice matching the movements of those close to you. You will soon notice that although the imitations seem obvious to you, those around you will be totally unaware of what you are up to.

In no way does the single technique of rapport sum up the benefits that NLP has brought to modern therapy, but it is the basis on which all therapy needs to stand; without rapport nothing else can be achieved.

Rapport can be gained in many ways, but by far the most useful in change therapy is the ability, through observing eye movements, to structure communication in any given individual's lead system.

Lead Systems

We each have preferences for how we like information presented to us. This is termed your **lead system**:

Some like to **SEE** what you mean . . .	**VISUAL**
Some like to **HEAR** your idea . . .	**AUDITORY**
Some like to **EXPERIENCE** or **FEEL** what you are talking about . . .	**KINESTHETIC**

We also have preferences for the way we evaluate and analyze information:

Some decide by how things **LOOK** to them . . .VISUAL
Some decide by how things **SOUND** to them . . **AUDITORY**
Some decide by how things **FEEL** to them . . .
                                    KINESTHETIC

Generally, people take in information and communicate in all three access modes. People can have one kind of preference for gathering information, and another kind for interpreting it. For example:

**LOOKING** *at a new car and then buying it because it* _**FEELS**_ *right.*

You will find that the client will be much more receptive if your ideas are presented in the way he or she prefers. So how, you might ask, do I know what a person's preference is? Fortunately, most people will give you cues that are often quite obvious when you know what you are looking for. Have you ever heard the term *"the eyes are the mirror to the soul?"* There is a great deal of truth to this statement. By watching the sequences of eye movement you will soon discover a pattern. By simply observing this pattern you will learn just how that person gets to *"yes"* -- the mystery is solved!

Eye Accessing

When people are in the process of communicating there are very definite physical signs that reflect how they are processing data.

When you ask someone a specific question he or she will begin to access memories, thoughts and ideas in order to formulate a response. His or her eyes will automatically move in a prescribed manner in order to create or retrieve the information. This eye movement will give you the information you need to respond back in the same lead system. Chances are good that your response will then be accepted as presented.

Physical Cues To Visual Processing

If you ask a question that requires the processing mode to think of a visual answer, the eyes will usually look up to the right or left.

Although there are exceptions, we can generally say that eyes looking up to the right or left will indicate that the person you are watching is processing visually. This does not necessarily mean, however, that this person is a visual access person. This will be covered in more detail later in this chapter.

In order to access visual processing it is necessary to ask a question that evokes a visual answer. A question that involves sound or feeling will not work.

VISUAL PREFERENCE
WORDS

* *I* **SEE** *what you mean.*
* *I can* **VISUALIZE** *it.*
* *That* **LOOKS** *good to me.*
* *Let me get a* **PERSPECTIVE***.*
* *I drew a* **BLANK***.*
* *I need to* **FOCUS** *in on that.*

The eyes tell you when the person is **LOOKING** for information or **VISUALIZING**. They may be accessing a remembered or constructed image or creating a picture. Eyes staring into space is also a sign of visual access.

Visualizing

Note: *Squinting or blinking can also indicate visualization, blinking can indicate punctuation as well.*

OTHER VISUAL ACCESS INFORMATION

BREATHING - *Shallow breathing high in the chest.*

TONE AND TEMPO - *High pitched, nasal tone and/or quick bursts of words in fast tempo.*

MUSCLE TONE - *Tension in the shoulders and stomach*

HAND AND ARM POSITIONS - *Finger pointing or arm extensions*

SKIN COLOR - *Pale or waning color*

Exercise

Building Visual Acuity

Directions:

Walk into a room of your house and look around for about ten seconds. Then walk into another room and write down everything that you remember seeing in that room.

Objective:

To increase visual acuity.
To increase observation skills.

AUDITORY PREFERENCE

When auditory processing is taking place the person's eyes will move toward the ears, either left or right. It is almost as if the brain is listening to the data.

WORDS

* *I* **HEAR** *what you are saying.*
* *Your idea* **SOUNDS** *good to me.*
* *Now that's an* **EARFUL**.
* *That story* **RINGS A BELL**.
* *I can't tell you where I've* **HEARD** *that before.*

Eye Movements

The eyes will tell you whether the person is recalling sounds or conversations, or constructing new ones. The eyes will usually look either directly to the right or left. Often *"shifty eyes"* are the eyes of an auditory access person. Also, when a person is looking down and to the left he or she is probably carrying on an internal dialogue; talking to himself or herself.

OTHER AUDITORY ACCESS INFORMATION

BREATHING PATTERN - *Even breathing in the diaphragm or with the whole chest, often with a prolonged exhale.*

TONE AND TEMPO - *Clear resonant tone and an even, rhythmic tempo.*

MUSCLE TONE - *Even muscle tension, minor rhythmic movement.s*

HAND AND ARM POSITIONS - *Hands and arms folded, Counting fingers, "Telephone" positions indicate internal dialogue.*

Exercise

Letting Go

1. *Think of a "negative" voice. Perhaps you will recall a voice from the past or a voice tone that is irritating to you. Imagine the pitch of that voice slowly going higher and higher until it is out of your range of hearing.*

2. *Think of that "negative" voice once again and then imagine the pitch going lower and lower until it is out of your hearing range.*

3. *When you bring the voice up are you able to hear it in the same way? If so repeat the process.*

The purpose of this exercise is to allow your mind to re-present the auditory information, in a new way, within your mind. If you give the mind all options, which means the option of going very low to a stop or very high until out of your hearing, then the brain will store it in the most appropriate way for you. Since the negative voice is not a voice that you would want to have in your future, the brain, knowing this and always making the best decision, will store it as *"hypermnesia,"* or out of your hearing. This is the selective ability to remember what you want to remember as you would want to remember it. In actuality, we do this all the time.

This technique of *"letting go"* is a very appropriate one to be used with many cases of unconscious overeating, such as someone who hears an internal voice from the past relating certain beliefs about food. A young woman by the name of "Alice" came in to see me for weight loss. She was a bright, enthusiastic and positive-minded young woman. But, somehow, once she started eating she just couldn't seem to stop until all of the food was gone.

I started by asking her just how she knew to continue eating the food on her plate. She stated that she knows in her mind when it is appropriate to stop, but sometime later realizes that all of the food has disappeared anyway. At this point, she had no idea how this was happening to her.

There were a couple of different strategies we could set into place. First, we could build a conscious approach of putting less food on her plate. This seemed to work rather well for awhile, except that no matter what amount of food was on her plate, whether dining in a restaurant or eating with friends, she would continue to eat until every bite was consumed.

Our next step was to use a process of modeling to discover the submodalities that were creating the eating behavior. What we discovered was that, deep within her mind, while she was consuming food, she would hear her mother, grandmother and other voices of authority from her childhood telling her, *"You must eat all of the food on your plate! There are children in Africa starving to death! How can you be so wasteful?!"*

As an adult, these voices are no longer relevant on the conscious level, but the unconscious mind doesn't discern. It utilizes all information as true. So Alice needed a way to re-present that information to the brain so that, whatever the intention, it could be met in a new way.

For Alice, the intention of the voice was a constant reminder that if she continued to eat until her plate was empty, her mother would discontinue admonishing her and would praise her for finishing her food. Therefore, she built a positive intention out of a negative behavior, or what turned into a negative behavior as she got older and her body's metabolism could no longer keep up.

Once the shift in the voice level was made by bringing the *"mother voice"* up to a high pitch to the point where she couldn't hear it, and then to the low point where it was dissipated, the brain was able to re-present that information in a way that was no longer relevant. The brain, now knowing that this event was no longer current or a pending situation, changed the way the voice was stored, rendering it irrelevant and Alice 's eating patterns changed allowing her to return to a healthy and normal weight.

Naturally, there were other techniques and patterns incorporated, but I do believe this was the key for Alice. If you can help someone find their key issue to overcoming a behavior pattern or an addiction, it can start a whole landslide of changes. So this technique is used to start the movement toward change, if not to accomplish the total change.

KINESTHETIC PREFERENCE

When accessing kinesthetically, you are accessing feelings. When a person is looking down and to the right he or she is usually getting in touch with feelings and emotions.

WORDS

* *I* **FEEL** *that we have made a great breakthrough.*
* *Let me get a* **HANDLE** *on what you're talking about.*
* *You've given me a* **SOLID** *understanding of your point.*
* *Please* **TACKLE** *this assignment as soon as you can.*
* *I haven't been able to* **GRASP** *the concept.*

Eye Movements

Eye movements for the Kinesthetic processor involve looking down and to the right. Eighty percent of all people tested looked down and to the right for accessing emotions and to judge their physical state.

OTHER KINESTHETIC ACCESS INFORMATION

BREATHING PATTERN - *Deep breathing in the lower stomach area.*
TONE AND TEMPO - *Low, deep voice quality, Voice may also be "breathy", Tempo is slow with long pauses*
MUSCLE TONE - *A great deal of movement and touching, Relaxed musculature indicates an inward contact with feelings*
HAND AND ARM POSITION - *Palms turned upward and arms bent and relaxed*
SKIN COLOR - *Increased, fuller color*

*"There is more to life
than increasing its speed."*

GANDHI

Auditory Digital

As explained in the auditory section, when self-talk is occurring and the person is accessing internal dialogue the eyes will move down and to your right. The term for this is auditory digital.

Identifying The Lead System

In general, you can identify the lead system of an individual by watching the first position the eyes move to when asked a neutral question.

It is possible for educators to determine an individual's learning strategy through eye access identification. By watching a student process a math problem, a teacher can determine that child's learning mode. With this information, the teacher is better equipped to help the student understand mathematics.

Much of NLP is based upon Bandler, Grinder and Robert Dilts' findings that people move their eyes in systematic directions depending upon the kind of thinking they are doing. In NLP these movements are called eye accessing cues. The Eye Accessing Chart indicates the kind of processing most people do when moving their eyes in a particular direction. A small percentage of people are reversed and will move their eyes in a mirror image to the chart. This is why calibration of each individual is so important. To calibrate is to watch and read an individual's external state through observable behavior cues which will relate to his or her internal state. People go through a variety of external changes during communication which are indicative of the internal responses. Examples are small gesture movements, a change in the breathing rate, voice tone and tempo changes, eye position changes, and changes in the body position such as a tilt of the head.

Remember, language is the poorest form of communication. It is essential to listen to the words spoken, but also pay attention to all the cues displayed by the individual. Remain focused on what is occurring externally.

The best way to use this chart is to imagine it superimposed over someone's face as if that person is looking back at you.

Eye Accessing Cues Chart

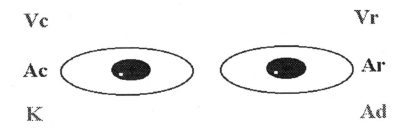

CONVERSATIONS AND MISCOMMUNICATIONS

As you become more aware of the non-verbal cues people give you, you will also notice how that person's verbal communication matches these outward signs. As you read over the following dialogue ask yourself: Who wins in this conversation? Do these two have rapport? What modes of communication are being used here?

SAL SALES: *"I would like you to LOOK at this proposal. I'm sure you will SEE how it will give your customers a new VISION of your company."*

CANDY CONSUMER: *"Yes, I FEEL there are some EXCITING points. But, I just can't get a HANDLE on how my clients will GRASP the concept."*

SAL SALES: *"Perhaps you don't SEE the entire PICTURE. I realize it APPEARS a little VAGUE right now, but if you will allow me to DEMONSTRATE what my company can do for your company, I know we will SEE EYE to EYE."*

CANDY CONSUMER: *"I need to GET IN TOUCH with my FEELINGS on this. Your proposal may change the entire FOUNDATION of our company. I need to FEEL COMFORTABLE with the whole concept. I'll TOSS IT AROUND in my mind and get back with you."*

SAL SALES Is: (✓) Visual ( ) Auditory ( ) Kinesthetic

CANDY CONSUMER is: ( ) Visual ( ) Auditory (✓) Kinesthetic

Will SAL sell his "VISION" to CANDY? ( ) Yes (✓) No

Who could benefit most from improved communication?
(✓) SAL ( ) CANDY ( ) Both[8]

It is not likely that SAL will sell his "VISION" or anything else to CANDY. It is as if they are speaking two entirely different languages.

Who could benefit most from improved communication?   Both. CANDY's job is to put her company in the best position for her customers and to help her company grow. By speaking the same language as the salesperson she can get the most complete information and make the best decision.

Of course, SAL's livelihood depends on his ability to communicate to the buyer. If SAL had spoken in CANDY's language she may very well have taken the time to get the details of his proposal. She may have been able to GET A HANDLE on his concept. These principles could mean the difference between success and failure.

How Can You Enhance Your Verbal Communication?

The following exercises will help you to understand how speaking in a person's *"language"* can help you to gain access to his or her bio-computer and to attain the results you want.

Start by imagining that you are a real estate sales person. Real estate agencies often report that the house clients describe and the one they actually buy are usually very different. The superior real estate sales person will first discover how a person processes data, thereby discerning the individual's buying strategy. The agent can then select a house that matches this buyer's "hidden" needs.

---

[8]Answers: Sal - Visual; Candy - Kinesthetic; Sell - No; Benefit - Both

The features a sales agent will want to emphasize:

For a VISUAL person? - Color, Look, Scenery.

For an AUDITORY person? - The quietness of the neighborhood. The sound construction. The nice conversations that the family could have.

For a KINESTHETIC person? - The solid foundation. This is a concrete investment. The firm offer.

Think about a certain place where you enjoy spending time. What is special about that place that makes you enjoy being there? Now think of a place where you just didn't like to be and could barely wait to leave. What was it about that place that was driving you away?

Clearly, atmosphere alone can make or break rapport.

Imagine that you are going on a first date and you want to make a good impression. What types of entertainment will this person enjoy?

For a VISUAL person? - A Movie; A night club with flashing lights; A scenic trip in the country.

For an AUDITORY person? - Listening to music; Going to a concert; A talk in a nice restaurant.

For a KINESTHETIC person? - Going for a walk; Exercising; Relaxing out in nature.

In building a relationship it is important to continuously access the other person's lead system to strengthen the bond and anchor to each other. Think about how getting the right gift could make the difference.

Listed below is the kind of special gift you might buy for a significant other for his or her birthday:

For a VISUAL person? - Watch; Picture; A flashy car.

For an AUDITORY person? - A record or tape; Concert tickets; A stereo.

For a KINESTHETIC person? - Comfortable clothing; Comfortable furniture; Loose fitting jewelry.

Establishing and maintaining communicative rapport is essential in any relationship. At times, we are placed into situations where rapport has been greatly diminished. This next question will help you to understand the use of lead systems to rebuild trust and rapport.

Listed below is how you might apologize to a significant other:

For a VISUAL person? - With flowers; Dinner in a classy restaurant; Doing something they can see.

For an AUDITORY person? I want you to hear me say I'm sorry, I hope you can hear me out, I'm sorry for what I've said.

For a KINESTHETIC person? - I know it's hard to handle but, I'm sorry; I'm sorry for grinding you the wrong way; Give a big hug while saying, "I'm sorry."

Anchoring

In the most general sense, an anchor is any stimulus which elicits a consistent response. One of the major breakthroughs in NLP is the discovery that a person can elicit a conditioned response in a single attempt once that response is intentionally linked to a touch, word, gesture or tone.

There are signals or signs that you automatically react to in one way or another, such as the STOP sign. There are also certain cultural anchors to which most members of a particular culture will respond. In the United States we have, the American Flag, the National Anthem, and Red/Yellow/Green Stop lights as examples.

Anchors from one's own personal history are also powerful. As examples: The smell of bread baking reminds you of Sunday visits to

Grandmother's house; the touch of leather against your hand reminds you of your favorite old leather jacket; or, the taste of cotton candy brings back memories from your first visit to the fair.

Music and songs are also anchors and often re-elicit sensory representations from the time when the tune was popular.

Advertising is possibly the best example of anchoring: *"The Real Thing,"* and *"Where's the Beef?"* are two good examples, and more recently, *"Food, Folks and Fun,"* or *"Just Gotta Have It."* These are just a few examples of how we are all intentionally conditioned into specific responses.

Anytime an individual is in an intense state and a specific stimulus is applied simultaneously, then the two -- stimulus and state -- become neurologically linked. In the future, when the stimulus is applied, the intense state will result.

Basic Anchoring Guidelines:

1. **Put yourself and/or the person to be anchored into the desired state.** Establish a Full Sensory Anchor, with all senses participating. Begin by recalling a situation or event which brings up the desired sights, feelings and sounds.

As an example, "Fred" was once a professional football player with a notable career behind him. After retirement, he wanted to become a successful salesman, but every time he picked up the phone he would start to feel as if he couldn't do it. He believed that he didn't have the skills or abilities to make the sale. He would ask himself, "Why am I even doing this?" He began to recall his lofty career in football and feelings of falling short overcame him. What he didn't realize is that a sales career is nothing shabby. Some of the richest people in the world are in sales. **I had Fred close his eyes and imagine a time, to the best of his ability, when he was doing something very well.** Fred had been a running back so I had him remember a time when he knew, without doubt, that if his play was called in the huddle, he would have every ability to carry it out. When Fred got into the football state, you could physically see the changes in his state. His face appeared visibly younger as a glow overcame him and a smile moved across his lips.

Now I could intensify the anchor. I asked him to step into the action. I began setting up the Five-Tupple,[9] which is an anchor with all five senses involved. I first had him visualize the experience internally. I had him imagine what was occurring around him, all that he could remember *seeing*. He could then begin to *hear* what he was saying to himself internally, and then what he was physically hearing at the time. Now he was able to access the *feelings* of the event. He began experiencing the feeling of the situation as if he were in that body again, breathing the way that he breathed at that time. I then had him add any *smells* or *tastes* that might have been present that would anchor him into that positive experience. Fred was now experiencing the event full sensory. He was seeing, hearing, feeling, smelling and tasting the incident fully. I have now set a full-sensory anchor, ready to be placed into Fred's future sales career.

2.   **At the height of the experience set the anchor.** The best anchor is a tactile one. This means to touch, preferably on the back of the hand or the shoulder. It is imperative that you explain the anchoring sequence to your clients before you ever touch them and that you anchor in a place that cannot possibly be misunderstood as an advance. Gauge the individual to find out whether it is appropriate to touch him or her.

There are, in fact, many different anchors. You can use tonal anchors with your own voice. For example, a minister who uses a certain emphasis while preaching to a congregation; such as using the word *"Jesus"* with conviction, is using a tonal anchor. Or, it could be the way a football or basketball coach uses the word *"breakdown."* By far, however, the best anchor for therapy purposes is the tactile one.

At the moment you notice the height of the experience you will reach over and touch the subject. After you have made the contact in an appropriate way and with an even pressure, you will release it completely.

3.   **After the anchor is set, that particular state is broken.** The subject is returned to full awareness of his surroundings. As an example suggestion, *"roll your eyes open and look around the room, noticing the room around you."* At times I will make an amusing comment or point out something noticeable within the room. It is also helpful to have your client shift the neurology of the body in some way so that the anchor is not linked to any other experience.

---

[9]Dilts. et al., Neuro-Linguistic Programming, 1980, Meta-Publications.

4.   Reactivate the anchor to test for responses: Skin color, breathing, body tension, posture, and movement. The test should elicit the original state for the anchor to be effective. Simply reach over and reactivate the anchor; touch the same place and then notice the reaction. If you need to strengthen the anchor, it is perfectly okay to build a stronger response at this time.

You will find that within the therapeutic patterns you will learn more about anchors and gain a better understanding of their usage. Anchoring is one of the primary tools of the NLP practitioner and will also be one of your major tools as you learn the patterns of Psycho-Linguistics.

Sub Modalities

All thinking takes place through one or more of the five sensory channels.   The face is a reflection of what is occurring internally.   Any sequence of images will produce the same external expression, whether through verbal or nonverbal behavior.   It is this processing of image types, and the expressions it elicits, that allows anchoring to be effective.   Submodalities are the internal characteristics in each modality (VAK) that together comprise the structure of an individual's experience.   Internal submodalities can produce external changes, and vice versa.

Example: Finding Submodalities

Question: *Go inside and find a positive memory. When you find it let me know.* When subjects verifies the positive memory move to next step.

Question: *Is the picture in color or black and white? Is it moving or still? Are you in the picture or watching it from a distance? Is there sound or is it silent?* You can ask any question that would have to do with the description of the experience or desired outcome to the sensory channels.

Finding and using submodalities can be much more sophisticated than this, as is demonstrated in many NLP books. However, after working with thousands of clients, I have come to the conclusion that submodality information is most useful in strategy intervention and modeling processes. That is not the focus of this text. Keep in mind that all the patterns of Psycho-Linguistics are designed to change, delete or distort the past information and to enhance, clarify and present the new information in a more appropriate light.

Again, the purpose of this book is not to be a text about NLP or hypnosis, but rather to outline the *Psycho-linguistic* patterns that are developed from the best of each. NLP has strongly influenced all areas of my therapeutic life and I would personally advise that if the patterns of *Psycho-Linguistics* interest you, and you would like to further your training within these realms, contact the NLP professional in your area, preferably one that has been trained through one of the recognized education programs such as NLP Comprehensive, NLP of Arizona or NLP of Ohio and/or demonstrates affiliation with the North American Association of Neuro-Linguistic Programming.

*"A retentive memory is a good thing,
but the ability to forget is the true token of greatness."*

ELBERT HUBBARD

"Everyone was surprised by the Master's update metaphor: Life is like a motor car . . . A motor car can be used to travel to the heights . . . But most people lie in front of it, allow it to run over them, then blame it for the accident."

Anthony de Mello
One Minute Wisdom
New York: Doubleday, 1988

Chapter Four

Accessing The Therapeutic Mind

In my early years as a therapist I began to ask the question: What would therapy sessions be like if I had the ability to tap into the minds of all other therapists who had ever performed the art of helping people? What if there was a universal mind to which I could *"tap in,"* so that I would somehow know exactly the right words to say at just the right time? If it did happen, how would I know that it had occurred? And what if, by happening just once, it could repeat itself every time I went into a therapeutic session? What if, in each session, I could tap into a potential within myself that could guide my conversations and my outcomes to elicit the best response for my client? What I found out was that all this could (and does) happen by a simple access into what I have come to call the ***therapeutic mind***.

There is a reason why you have chosen to pick up this book and read it at this very moment. It is because you have a desire. This desire will vary from person to person, but for most it is either a desire to help yourself, to help others, or, as a practicing therapist, to find fresh, new ideas for enhancing your current techniques.

There is a very real way to access all of these possibilities. In hypnosis training they teach you to move into a state called *self-hypnosis*. NLP practitioners call it entering a *state of mind*. In Silva Mind Control they direct you to *go to level*. I believe it is most appropriately termed the *therapeutic mind*. Your mind works best when you are specific. There is a specific place in each and every one of us that has chosen a therapeutic profession -- it is a place for compassion, for helping people, for guiding others to solutions and well-being. This *therapeutic mind* is the part of you that needs to read through this text and then review the information to ensure a natural flow of knowledge whenever you need it.

There are some simple guidelines for tapping into the *therapeutic mind* that will allow for the freedom and flexibility of the non-contextual Psycho-Linguistic patterns. I teach every therapist that even though I am teaching specific guidelines for success, they must be flexible enough to create an effectiveness with each individual personality. When people sit across from you and begin to tell you their outcomes, desires and wants, you must be adaptable enough to create new patterns and techniques.

Plan to take what you read in this book and combine it with what you have read elsewhere, what you have seen in any film, heard on any tape, or learned at any seminar, and be willing to use all that you know to create your own patterns for success. This kind of creativity will keep you actively involved in your therapy sessions and, most importantly, will make being a therapist fun and adventurous.

When helping others to achieve change, it is necessary to put yourself into a receptive state. This is the state that I call the *therapeutic mind*. Most people who get into professions that are geared toward helping others, whether through hypnosis, psychology, nursing, or Neuro-Linguistic Programming, have a deep caring for people. To be successful with others who have changes to make and problems to overcome, it is important that you get into that place of caring.

The following suggestions are written for you. Simply take a moment to read through them and then begin to use them in your daily life and activities. See how they affect your relations with others.

Guidelines For Tapping Into
The Therapeutic Mind

1. **Notice:** How does your brain operate when you have all of the information you need to say exactly what you need to say as you need to say it?

2. **Notice:** What it's like when you are sitting and talking with someone with whom you feel comfortable? And what happens if you become aware of his or her breathing and begin to mirror that breathing? At times you will mirror the breathing consciously and other times it will happen automatically. This will begin to set up a bond of rapport between the two of you. Your dialogue will begin to flow freely and unconsciously. You will find yourself speaking as the person breathes out each time.

3. **Notice:** How your subject's eyes move. Is this person visual, auditory or kinesthetic?

4. **Process:** How effective you will be with all these techniques as you learn to put them in their right sequence and begin to access that place known as *rapport.*

By putting together a series of events that will take place like a check list and occur automatically, you are now incorporating the *therapeutic mind.* As you check off the items in your mind, you will feel confident and prepared to do just what is needed. It is recommended that you place these suggestions on index cards and read them as often as possible so that you are consistently placing yourself into the state of *therapeutic mind.*

Let's take this a little further. Say an elderly woman comes to you to stop smoking after a 45 year habit. Her life and motivations are much different from yours. However, through the use of these techniques you will begin to see the world through her eyes, yet retaining the integrity of your own ideas and visions. In other words, you view the client's world, or her map of it, and help her to plot a course of success to where she wants to go--which is not necessarily where *you* want her to go. Always remember that she came to you because you have techniques and tools which she believes will give her the ability to attain her goal.

In other words, keep a positive attitude about your client. Realize that all behaviors are positive. Behind every behavior there is a positive intention that your client is attempting to accomplish. Until now, however, it has been in an inappropriate way. Your job is to help her, through the visual, auditory and emotional channels, to change the way that she responds to life. She needs a change that will fulfill her positive intention and convince her that, once and for all, absolutely and positively, it will improve her world.

While helping every client to make it through his or her day-to-day activities in new ways, it is imperative that you focus on behavior changes that are equally as immediate and appropriate. This means to help your client function within his or her existing world and to move through experiences with a positive mental attitude and with relaxation in mind and body.

From here you will take your client into the future. Thoughts of the days, weeks and months to come with this new, positive attitude should now be placed within the mind. This new perception of the future, along with the forecasting ability of the mind, will bring all the solutions into view. Remember always that the power to change is within each person. You, as a therapist, hold the golden key for yourself alone. All the clients who walk through your door already have their own golden key and the potential to change. Clients are paying you because you can teach them how to use their keys and how to access change. It is your job to show these people the power of their keys, how to use them and then to hand the keys over. You are empowering your clients to go out into the world and create a better future.

Therapeutic Rapport

The ability to ask the right questions, to build an awareness of the person's position and then to become one with him or her is known as *therapeutic rapport.* Once this rapport is established the client can more readily be led into a positive and more compelling state.

Therapeutic rapport is accomplished in a variety of ways. The most widely used method involves breathing with the same rhythm as another person. After you breathe like someone for a while, he or she will begin to feel a connection with you. It will be the feeling of *bonding*, but it will not be conscious. This unconscious bonding is the most important contact between you and your client.

Another way to build this common bond is to use the same lead system as your client. Whether that system is visual, auditory, or kinesthetic (emotional), even if it is different from your own, it is the most familiar to that individual. For example, a 25 year-old man has come to you because he has decided to start a college program, but is having difficulty recalling the information he is learning. His lead access is kinesthetic. This young man would probably find it very difficult to describe his problem to you. What would happen if you began to ask him questions using his lead system? You would be able to help him access his own bio-computer because you will be in the position of controlling the conversation. He will automatically begin accessing through his feelings. You have not only developed rapport with this young man, but you are also in a position to elicit the information you need and to direct the session to his outcomes. Realize that there is a difference between controlling a person and controlling the session. You, as a therapist, can only control the session.

An individual's own tone and tempo is also a very familiar place within. If you begin using the same rate of speech and voice level, it will tap into a comfortable place inside of that person. In most cases, when an individual speaks rather quickly he or she is accessing a visual mode of communication. If an individual's cadence of speech is rapid, and you respond with that same tempo and tone, the brain will hear it and assimilate it as if it was said within his or her own mind. *(Review Chapter Two.)*

Body language is a familiar term today, but most people don't realize the effect that a mutual body posture can have when building rapport in communication. If your client, say a young female who is not familiar with discussing her behaviors with a stranger, is sitting with her legs crossed and her hands clamped tightly in her lap, you can be certain that she does not yet feel comfortable with you. How do you persuade this young woman to open up to you? You can start out by positioning your body in her same posture and crossing your body in the same way. As the conversation goes on, begin to open your body up and uncross your limbs. More often than not, she will follow your lead and uncross her posture as well. Once her posture is open, she is more readily able to share with you and will be receptive to the information you are now going to impart. She is now able to accept the new, positive information that she is paying you to receive.

These techniques will build therapeutic rapport; a level of trust that needs to occur for the person to accept what you are saying and to place you in control of the session.

Therapeutic Ethics

When using mind technology, whether it's hypnosis, Neuro-Linguistic-Programming, or psychology, there is an element of power that you have over the other person--it is the command over the communication. You will be able to persuade people, both consciously and unconsciously, to make changes to their thinking--sometimes without their awareness that the change has been made. However, the same rules apply with Psycho-Linguistics, or any other method of persuasion, as they do to hypnosis; *no one will be made to do anything they would not otherwise do.*

If you have picked up this book with the intention of gaining skills for controlling others in less than positive ways, then this is not the mind technology for you. These techniques are designed for enhancement of the personality and you will find no brain-washing methods within these pages. All patterns work best when the person is motivated by positive outcomes. I emphasize that a therapist does not have control over the other person, but does hold the ability to control the situation. Because you are learning to use and master the vocabulary, as well as helping the other person to access information within their mind, you surely are aware that there is an element of control. But you are controlling the communication which is only effective by virtue of the response it elicits. Success lies within the communication taking place between you and the subject. If success is occurring within that conversation, you can see, feel and hear that success taking place. As you master the art of communication, success will soon become a day-to-day experience for you. You will be setting up such a powerful program within your mind that each day it will grow stronger than the day before.

This is the true promise of your mind--to take in all information, absorb it, calculate it, and then formulate a new future. This process will even carry over into your dreams so that every night as you drift off into sleep, in that state of dreamy drowsiness, your powerful mind is forecasting your next day, the next week and even the next months to come. It validates all information and puts it into motion for you.

Most Probable Future

The most probable future is the future that is most likely to happen if all events and circumstances remain on their present course. There are many reasons for keeping the word *"why"* out of a therapy session when utilizing these patterns. The main reason is that the question *"why"* gives the client access into an emotional response or into other unnecessary programs; the proverbial *"bucket of worms."* If you want to spend hours listening to your clients explain all of their problems and situations, then ask the question *"Why?"*

The reality is that the mind doesn't really care to worry about the patterns of the past. In fact, the mind is an expert at the past and the reasons *"why."* What the client's mind does need to know is specifically what is going to be done, how is it going to get done, when will it be taken care of, with whom, and so on. The brain is a servo-mechanism. It only knows how to achieve goals. As you place the goals in the mind in a positive and appropriate way, the brain fills with awe and wonder and begins to build an expectancy. In that building of expectancy the brain will activate the thoughts of the mind into motion. In actuality, no one really knows the full effects that the mind can have on the body or its will. You are empowering the mind for action; setting up a most probable future in which all desirable outcomes are fulfilled.

"Why" is not a word of empowerment. *"Why"* is an out. It is an excuse which is not used in any therapy session at our centers or in any other therapeutic session that has a positive outcome.

Remember that you are seeking solutions and your mind and every client's mind wants to generate them. Whether you are using these techniques to help yourself or as a therapist for others, you need to place yourself and other people into a point of power. When you empower people around you, you become more powerful.

Outcomes for Hypnotic Rapport

In building therapeutic rapport, ethics and control, there is one essential element that must be present, and that is the need for outcomes. Your mind needs outcomes for it to work properly, and it needs to know that those outcomes are going to fulfill some underlying intention.

The following suggestions are known as the *"patterns of hypnotic rapport."* There is no need for you to answer them consciously, but you may write them down, or say them out loud. Simply allow your mind to drift and wander as you ponder on each of the questions.

1. **Unconscious Mind**, what could I do today in a simple way that can improve my life and help me reach my goals?

2. **Unconscious Mind**, will you be willing to bring these new behaviors and attitudes into reality so I can benefit from using them through the days, weeks and months to come . . . so that I might use them and integrate them into my world on a permanent and lasting basis?

3. **Unconscious Mind**, will you guide me through a process of viewing how often I will need to display these behaviors before they become an active part of my personality? Will it happen today? Next week? Or a month from today?

4. **Unconscious Mind**, is there any reason I shouldn't make these changes?

5. **Unconscious Mind**, what stops me from making these changes without your help? Can you begin a process of re-education that will retrain the past to accept the bright and compelling future you hold for me?

6. **Unconscious Mind**, what resources do I have available to use in making this change? How can I begin to use them through the days, weeks, and months to come to get what I want out of life on a day-to-day basis?

7. **Unconscious Mind**, what are the positive benefits of my allowing this change to occur? What will be the positive outcome for all of those around me?

8. **Unconscious Mind**, is there any part of my personality that doesn't agree with this change? If there is, Unconscious Mind, would you begin a process of creative possibilities that would allow that part to do what it can to move in a harmonious and positive way with me into the future? What would that look like, sound like, and feel like when all parts of my consciousness are working together to help me achieve my goals?

9. **Unconscious Mind**, what is going to happen to convince me that the changes have been made? . . . So that every night as I drift off into dreams, memories and deep sleep, you will guide me into solutions in my life to awaken with a strong, positive attitude that will improve with time? What would it be like if it just happened?

10. **Unconscious Mind**, I want to thank you for being there for me, for beating my heart and building my body. I know what you do for me is no small thing, but it is very special, and can be done in an easy way. Thank you again, because I know that each time I go to this level of the mind my abilities will improve.

As you read over these ten questions, you will notice how each statement can be re-worded to become outcome questions you can ask someone else.

1. What would you like to attain from Psycho-Linguistics?
2. When would you like to have these changes?
3. How often will you need to display these behaviors to convince you that you have made a change?
4. Is there any reason you shouldn't make this change?
5. What stops you from making this change on your own?
6. Have you ever made a similar change?
7. What are the positive benefits of making this change?
8. Is there any part of you that doesn't want the change?
9. Is there any place you don't want the change?
10. What will need to occur during the processes for you to make the change?

Note that as the therapist you must be convinced that you have all the necessary information to guide your client to a successful change.

Notice that the above questions all begin with: **What? Where? How? When? With Whom?** Because it is so essential for success, I reiterate here, the word *"why"* should be eliminated from any therapeutic session. You will find it nowhere in this list or any of the patterns of non-contextual therapy. The reason *"why"* has nothing to do with any change, and will in no way move that person toward success in the future.

On the other hand, if you elicit how success will be accomplished, when it will occur and with whom . . . you are setting up the mind's process for success. If you focus on success, your chances of achieving success are much greater.

Impact Words

What are they and how do you get them?

Do you remember how, as you grew out of childhood and into adolescence, you developed that one special friendship or a close knit group of friends? Chances are that your circle of friends developed an exclusive language code involving words and phrases that were unique to the members of that circle. These words began to develop a special meaning for you and began to have a certain *"impact"* on your consciousness.

Through life's experiences, we all progressively develop a structure of belief. Within this belief system there are certain words that have a special meaning for us. My impact words are most likely very different from yours, and yours are very different from your neighbor's. These are the individual's own set of words that will have the greatest impact on his or her consciousness.

There are questions that will elicit the client's impact words and help to ensure the safe fulfillment of his or her outcomes while keeping in mind the proper balance or ecology.

1.   WHAT HAS TO BE PRESENT IN A JOB FOR YOU TO ENJOY IT?

You will soon be putting your client's mind to "work." In order to do it successfully you must know what the individual's underlying positive motivation is and how it works. Then, during the session, you can tap into a pre-existing motivation strategy by using the motivating impact words. All suggestions and programming techniques can be structured with the use of impact words so that they make sense to, and have an impact on, the person receiving the programming.

2. WHAT HAS TO BE PRESENT IN A RELATIONSHIP FOR YOU TO ENJOY IT?

The importance of asking about relationships is simple. When the behavior changes are made, your client will have a new relationship with his or her inner self. For the new programs to feel right they must be stored with the positive relationship programs of the past. Using the relationship impact words within the suggestions will allow the new programs the respect needed to be accessed and used.

3. WHAT HAS TO BE PRESENT IN A HOBBY FOR YOU TO ENJOY IT?

Your client has come to you because he or she wants the new programs to be easy and accomplished with a minimal effort. How easy is it to accomplish a task when it feels as if you are doing something you enjoy? The client is not only using the new program, but is enjoying using it as well!

4. HOW DO YOU KNOW WHEN YOU HAVE DONE A GOOD JOB?

Most people will have some method of judging information; whether it is good, bad or indifferent. By gathering this information you can set up the suggestions to move along a time line of success with which the individual is comfortable. In other words, because this person must be capable of believing that success is possible, you are setting up guidelines within his or her belief structure. The response to this question will also let you know whether your client uses an internal or external acceptance of information. Which means, does this individual know that he or she is doing well, or does this acceptance need to come from someone else?

Impact words are those that hold a special meaning for a particular person. These are the words that are used with every client to instill a deep level of trust and rapport because they have a direct impact on his or her psyche.

You will also find that impact words are the basis for the modeling process. This is the process of watching someone demonstrate a behavior and learning from the internal and external cues how to imitate that behavior so you can get the same result. The patterns of Psycho-Linguistics were modeled from a group of innovative researchers who named their discovery Neuro-Linguistic Programming. These are people who have spent their entire careers modeling the people around the world who excel at their profession. With Psycho-Linguistics you are taking their discoveries of success and motivation into the life of your client.

What Is Ecology?

Webster's defines Ecology as *"a science concerning the interaction of organisms and their environment."* For the purpose of therapy, we will define Ecology as the science concerning the interaction between the thinking process and its environment. The environment represents the total well-being of the person. If this person makes this change, is there going to be a greater or a lessening effect in the self-image, self-concepts or beliefs? Is anything going to be lost by making this change? When making changes you must look at the ecology to make sure that all modifications are upgrades in consciousness, upgrades in the person's life and experience.

Within all change technology, there is no more important factor than that the shift happen at the right time and at the right pace. This is one of the basic principles of Psycho-Linguistics; always look at all the angles.

1. If this change happens are there any negative or less than positive side effects?

2. When this change happens will you need any further training to keep you from harm?

3. Are there any special precautions that you should take now that this change has been made?

These are questions that would bring any ecology questions to the surface. As the answers are given you can begin to use your creative mind to guide the individual through the process.

As an example, if you want to help someone overcome a fear of water you would want that person to first agree to attend swimming lessons so that he or she would have the ability stay afloat in the water. For someone who has no swimming ability, the fear of water is well founded. The point is to plan success on all levels so that there are no miscommunications. Always look at every angle.

Utilizing Your Therapeutic Mind

As you learn to access the therapeutic mind, it may seem as if you have more power than others. The truth is that, in a sense, this power is real. You have an *ability*, therapeutic in nature, and there is a *response* that goes along with it--*responsibility*. The more you generate powerful and positive patterns for others, the more powerful and positive you will become. Your life will begin to flow in harmony, it will change in inexplicable ways and become enhanced. People will seek you out for counsel and for speaking engagements.

First and foremost, however, you must understand the laws of the therapeutic mind. Transference is a common occurrence in this world; such as the transference from an employee to the boss or from a patient to the doctor. All transference needs to be superimposed or changed. I look at transference as an opportunity to shift disempowerment to empowerment through the process of building a bright and compelling future. I am continually building a future in which my clients, every one of them, can look out of their window in the morning and say, "Aah, it's a beautiful day; I know it's a perfect day for me to be successful!" Whether they know this consciously or unconsciously is irrelevant. The most important thing to know is that they are now becoming addicted to the world and to the life they have chosen to live--a life of abundance, expectancy and filled with positive changes--for change is truly the nature of all things.

So now you know, the real control is in *allowing* the superconscious mind to do what it does best. There is a power that is far superior to the conscious mind and it is the job of the hypnotherapist to prove that this power exists. It has always been there for each client who has walked through the doors of a therapy office. Most people will be unaware that they have ever entered into the hypnotic state, but they will see, hear and experience the changes upon awakening. The element of control is in helping your client to notice that part which has always been there inside, but that he or she has thus far been unable to experience in life. You are going to prove that this greater part exists and that within it lies success.

"People hate me because I am a multifaceted, talented, wealthy, internationally famous genius."

JERRY LEWIS

Chapter Five

Techniques For Altered States

There is an unlimited variety of techniques for placing someone into an altered state. Watch a good salesman sometime. He has Mrs. Buyer driving that car or trying out that vacuum cleaner before she knows what hit her. She was put into an altered state, without ever knowing it happened.

Any technique used with a person to either test or gather information is placing that individual into an altered state. It is the purpose of this chapter to give you tangible and usable techniques to guide yourself or another into the altered state of hypnosis. The ensuing chapters will cover a variety of techniques, but in no way is this the limit of approaches that the trained therapist will have available to use. For each therapist there are no limitations. Each of these techniques are designed to work in a non-contextual format. In other words, they can work for any area of change or enhancement desired. These methods can be interwoven, one with another. I never limit my client's success to one method or technique. I believe that for each individual there is a tapestry for change . . . it is my job to weave together his or her *new* concept of reality.

Eye Roll Trance Technique

Although the Eye Roll Trance is usually a part of the testing process it can also be used for integrating a selective state. Therefore, this method is included as part of this section.

First have the subject roll the eyes upward. Place your finger on the forehead at the hairline to give the subject a focal point.

Give the suggestion: *Roll your eyelids down.*

Suggest: *Once the eyelids are closed imagine that the muscles and tendons are going loose, limp and completely relaxed . . . to the point where* *they won't open at all. You realize that they could open, but you are imagining that they won't open at all.*

Suggest: *Relax all body parts by allowing a wave of relaxation starting from your facial muscles and tendons, moving down through your body, through the scalp and to the neck, down to the shoulders and arms all the way to the tips of the fingers . . . in the chest, abdomen and back, allowing all inner organs to go loose, limp and totally relaxed, all the way down through the hips, thighs and knees, and, out the bottom of the feet . . .*

Suggest: *From here you can come back to fully awakened consciousness but only as slowly as you are able to incorporate this level of relaxation into your life . . . and this is so . . . Take all the time you need . . .*

Progressive Relaxation Technique

This technique is best used with people who take inferred suggestions. These are the people who need to be led all the way through the hypnotic experience.

I'm going to ask you to close your eyes . . . and begin to feel the muscles and tendons around the eyes. Use your mind to make them tighter and tighter . . . and as they get tighter and tighter, just tighten them so tight with your mind and with your physical body . . . and then just let them go.

Allow a wave of relaxation to move from your eye muscles and tendons down through your body. Become aware of the scalp now . . and use your mind and your body to tighten up your entire face, your scalp and your neck. Tighten them as much as possible . . . tighter and tighter now . . . and then hold it . . . hold on to all the tension of the day . . . hold on to all frustration . . . hold on to all anxiety . . . and with your muscles tight take in as much air as you can . . . and now let it all out . . . let out all of the tightness. Allow the tightness within the scalp, the facial muscles and tendons, and the eyes to let go. Let the body fall loose and limp and relaxed like a handful of rubber bands . . . going loose, going limp, and going completely and totally relaxed.

It is from here that I want you to move your awareness to your hands. Allow your hands to grip down into a fist . . . making your hands tighter and tighter . . . hold on to all frustration for a moment . . . and then just let your hands go, dropping them loose, limp and completely relaxed. Allow a wave of gentle relaxation to move freely from the very tips of your fingers up and through the body . . . allowing you to feel a passive state of relaxation . . . knowing that each and every time you use this procedure you are going to go deeper and further into the state of relaxation.

It is from here that I want you to once again grip down with your fists and make them tighter and tighter . . . and allow the forearms to get tight . . . and the upper arms now. . . all the way to the shoulders . . . making them tighter and tighter. Think of all the things that might anger you. I want you to try to hold on to that anger . . . try to hold on . . . and then just let it all go. . . breathing out . . . letting go. Allow a gentle wave to massage all muscles, all tendons and all nerve endings . . . as you begin to feel a new feeling . . . perhaps a tingling sensation in your hands . . . a lightness or a heaviness. Whatever it is that you are feeling it is uniquely yours. No two people feel the same in a state of relaxation. Allow yourself to go deeper and further with each and every breath that you take.

Move your awareness now down to the bottom of your feet. From the bottom of your feet begin to tighten all the muscles within the feet and ankles . . . tighten all the muscles within the calves and shins . . . tighten all the muscles within the knees and thighs . . . all the way to the hips and buttocks. Tighten them now . . . tighter and tighter . . . and hold for the mental count of three . . . two . . . one . . . let them go now . . . breathing out . . . just let them go. Feel the wave of relaxation now moving into your body. Your physical body is now learning about the power of relaxation. It's learning to relax completely and deeply with the sound of my voice and through the power of your own mind.

So, now tightening once again starting with the hands, the feet and the top of the head . . . tightening all the muscles from the hands, the arms, the shoulders, the feet, the calves, all the way up through the knees, the thighs, the buttocks, the head area . . allow that tightness to move into the chest . . . and feel the chest and abdomen muscles tightening . . . the back muscles tightening . . . tighten every muscle in the body and hold it to the mental count of three . . . two . . . one . . . take a deep breath now . . . hold it . . . hold it . . . and now just breathe it out . . . let it go. Let it go and feel the body sinking into a state of relaxation . . . a state of deep and total body relaxation.

It is from here that your body is going to learn to go deeper as we go through this process one more time. When I ask you to tighten the muscles, tighten them even tighter than you have done before. Starting with the hands, the feet, the scalp, feel the body begin to tighten all muscles, all tendons, all nerve endings . . . tightening all muscles in the abdomen, chest and back area. Begin to breath in deeply now . . . tighter and tighter . . . and breathing in . . . hold on to that breath . . . counting now three . . . two . . . one . . . just let it out now, let it go.

As you let it go now allow your body to sink into a deep rhythmic state. You're doing perfectly. You can now use your mind to scan your physical body to find any area that is still tight. Using your mind, imagine that all muscles, all tendons, all nerve endings in that area are going loose, limp and completely relaxed. You can now imagine that with each breath you are breathing in the word **relaxation**, *and you are breathing out all in harmony . . . and now you are breathing in deeply the word of* **peace** . . . *mental peace . . . mental clarity . . . mental calmness. . .*

Begin to think in your mind of a gentle pond. This pond is gentle and peaceful and full of vegetation. The sun is just coming up and across the pond there is a beautiful deer. The deer is going to the pond for a drink of water . . . and you're just sitting there . . . relaxing . . . watching it all. You can notice the birds flying . . . and the wonderful sound that they make as they communicate to each other.

As you relax here you will find that your mind will drift off to a more beautiful place . . . it will be your perfect place of relaxation. My voice will now pause and you will continue to go deeper and deeper into relaxation . . . in fact, the deeper you go the better you will feel upon awakening. So, each and every time that you use this technique you are going to feel better and better about yourself. Each and every time that you use this technique your ability to relax the muscles and tendons of your body will come to you more easily and in a more progressive fashion. Soon, and very soon indeed, you will simply need to close your eyes with the intention or idea of going into relaxation and instantly, automatically, without a conscious thought, your body will mirror this state of relaxation and, in fact, take you even deeper. Deeper and deeper each and every time with more and more positive benefits upon awakening. The positive benefits will increase and intensify into your life, making positive, bright and compelling changes to your future. Changes that you will be willing to take part in upon awakening. My voice will now pause . . . (2-3 minutes) . . .

As you become aware of my voice once again, I want you to become aware of the state of your body's relaxation at this time . . . for you are going to carry this relaxation into your life. So, begin to think about where you would want relaxation or the ability to be calm and at peace with yourself. Begin to think of the next day . . . the next week . . . and the next month to come. For soon, the days will become weeks . . . and the weeks will become months and the months will become years. Soon you will be thinking back over time at all of the changes you made. Changes that were instantaneous and automatic, relaxing and progressive through the rest of your life.

It is from here that I am going to count from one to five . . . at the count of five your eyes will open and you will become wide awake, feeling fine and in perfect health, feeling better than ever before as if you have just received a deep peaceful and rhythmic sleep. It is from this perfect place of relaxation that you will return into your life with a positive mental attitude about yourself, your world, and your ability to relax in the future.

One . . . hearing the sounds around you more fully. Two . . allowing the blood to flow freely with a warmth of circulation. Three . . . personality intact, perfect and powerful in every way. Four . . . with a perfect memory and recall of all that you saw, heard and experienced so that you can benefit from all of the creativity. And, Five . . . eyes open, wide awake and in perfect health . . . knowing that every day, in every way you are getting better, better and better . . . and this is so.

"Thought takes man out of servitude, into freedom."

HENRY WADSWORTH LONGFELLOW

Safe Place Technique

The Safe Place Technique is designed to help your subjects feel that they are in a safe place. The subject is guided to a safe haven where hidden blocks within their consciousness can be uncovered. These blocks might otherwise prevent the subject from utilizing the hypnotic skills or their mental potential to its fullest.

I have also arranged this technique so that the therapist can use it in accessing the therapeutic mind. If, as the therapist, you are reading the script for your own growth and advancement, simply add in the sections divided with [ ].

Just close your eyes now . . . and with your eyes closed imagine the eye muscles and tendons going completely relaxed. Just take a deep breath in, and as you breathe in deeply begin to imagine the eye muscles going loose, limp and relaxed. As you breathe out with a sigh, let all of the tension of the day out . . . just let it all go now.

Because you have already been through the hypnotic processes many times before, you're going to find that your unconscious mind has already begun the process of relaxation . . . so focus your attention and awareness on the powerful flow of relaxation. Become aware of your hands and feet and allow them to go loose, limp and completely and totally relaxed . . . just let go . . . let yourself go. Become aware of the powerful flow of relaxation as it enters into your arms and legs . . . aware of the physical body and its relaxation . . . for the deeper you relax the more benefit you will receive . . . and the more benefit you receive the deeper you will go. Allow this flow and powerful feeling of relaxation to flow into the torso . . . into the buttocks . . . the pelvic area . . . up into the chest and abdomen. Allow all inner organs . . . all inner systems . . . all cells . . . to go loose, to go limp and to go completely and totally relaxed . . . just letting go. Become aware of the beating of your heart . . . rhythmic and natural. Become aware of your breathing . . . slow and rhythmic. Take this time to connect the breath . . . breathing in . . . and breathing out. Now you can allow that powerful flow of relaxation to move into the neck and head area. And, your entire body is now more deeply relaxed than ever before.

Imagine that a crystalline white light is now coming down from the very center of the universe. Allow this brilliant white light to move down through the top of your head and into your heart. Allow it to now radiate out from the heart to the very tips of your fingers . . . to the very ends of your feet . . . and to the top of your head. Begin to imagine that you are creating a powerful magnetic aura around you . . . a powerfully strong magnetic aura that allows only that which is good to flow to you . . . and only that which is good to flow from you.

Your powerful mind can now allow you to float back in time. Imagine that you are going back in time to a place where you felt safe. Feeling safe may be an image in your mind . . . a picture of a place where you felt very safe. It could be a sound, a certain type of music or someone's voice talking to you. Or, this safe place could simply be a feeling . . . a feeling coming from within you. Whatever this safe place is for you, allow yourself to move into it and let it grow within your body as if each and every breath could allow it to grow and build within you. Allow this safe place to become a part of your very existence right here and now. Through the power of your mind and imagination this safe place is resonating around you as your magnetic aura. You are safe. [In this **safe place you are able to use your hypnotic skills and your therapeutic skills to help yourself and to help others. In fact, you will find that all you have ever seen, all that you ever heard and all that you have ever experienced is now acceptable and accessible to your mind. You will use it when you need it the most whether it is with yourself or with a client in the future.]**

Take this time to create this safe place by breathing in as I count down from three to one. With each descending number just let that safe place resonate out and fill the room . . . three . . . two . . . one. Imagine that with each and every breath the safe place is now growing and building . . . to fill your body, the room, and even the building that you are now in. And it slowly begins to fill the city. Your safe place is growing so that wherever you go you now know that you have access to your higher mind. From the city to the state . . . from the state to the country . . . from the country to the world . . . and now from the world to the solar system . . . and from the solar system to the universe . . . and now to the omni-verse. Allowing your powerful mind . . . through the use of your imagination . . . to expand and explore . . . transmitting and receiving the higher thought of your own being.

My voice will now pause and as I pause the seconds will become hours, the hours will become days and the days will become weeks. It is here that whatever change you may be working on, or whatever you want to accomplish today will happen. When my voice returns it will not startle you at all. In fact it will place you into a deeper and more relaxed place in consciousness . . . and this is so. (Pause for one minute.)

. . . As you once again become aware of my voice, you realize that you will bring this safe place back with you . . . back from the omni-verse . . . into the universe . . . into this solar system . . . into this world . . . into this country . . . into this state . . . into this city . . . into this building . . . into this body . . . and begin to breathe energy into your body as I count from one to five. At the count of five your eyes will open and you will become wide awake, feeling fine and in perfect health, feeling better than ever before . . . as I count . . . one, coming back into the room . . . two, feeling the energy pouring through you with each and every breath, revitalizing every cell, every system and every organ . . . three, feeling better and better about yourself [and about your skills as a hypnotist] . . . four, becoming more and more positive about information as you have read or experienced it . . . and, five, eyes open, wide awake, feeling fine and in perfect health, feeling better than ever before . . . as if you have just received a deep, peaceful and relaxing sleep . . . and this is so.

These are the basic types of induction techniques and are a great starting point for guiding yourself or your clients into the altered state. It should be noted, however, that there are any variety of induction techniques, many of which will be integrated through the following processes. As you become more comfortable with the induction process you may want to use your own creativity to develop methods for initiating an altered state. You will soon discover how easily the Psycho-Linguistic techniques can be mixed, matched, and individualized for any personality.

"In skating over thin ice our safety is in our speed."

RALPH WALDO EMERSON

Trance Management

So, here you are. You have this person in an altered state and deeply relaxed. Now What? When discussing trance management it must be noted that very deep trance states of hypnosis are not necessary for change to occur. In most cases it is better if the subject is in a light state of relaxation. Many readers may find this last statement surprising, especially those who have taken previous hypnotherapy training. Too often the goal of a hypnosis course is to teach you how to get the subject into the deepest trance state possible, and then rate your success on this basis. The hypnotic "state" is only a segment of an entire process, and is certainly not your only, or even primary, objective. The techniques that you will find in this chapter can be accomplished in either a deep or light trance state.

Less than 10% of the population is the responsive deep-trance type subject. If only deep-trance subjects were able to use hypnosis, we would be out of business. In truth, almost anyone could get the highly suggestible type of subject to respond. Stage hypnosis, which is often difficult for people to understand, is a perfect example. Indeed, the hypnotist is giving the suggestions, but it is the deep and very suggestible subjects who perform the incredible feats. These people are what is known as *somnambulistic*, which means "sleepwalker." These sleepwalkers are capable of feats which would otherwise be impossible or extremely difficult for anyone to perform. A full-body catalepsy is a good example. The body is made stiff and rigid as if it is an iron bar. It is then easily lifted and placed between the backs of two chairs. Some stage hypnotists have even been known to stand on the cataleptic subject or to break bricks placed on the torso of the stiff body. I do not recommend either of these methods as they can be dangerous and are not necessary to prove the mind's ability.

In my life around hypnosis, I have personally met hundreds of hypnotists and therapists. Frankly, I am often amazed by the unusual and illogical approaches that so many believe is the right way to achieve change. Somehow, the techniques of hypnosis have fallen short for many. They seem to feel that if they can get a person into a deep altered state they will miraculously access a change. It is indeed true that hypnosis is a "conviction phenomena" in many ways, but simply getting the subject to an altered state certainly does not guarantee success in making a change.

The techniques to come are a synthesis of my experience with NLP, hypnosis, and many other mind technologies. During my research, I came to a definitive conclusion that in all trance sessions it is important to establish a way of communicating with the subject once he or she is in the altered state. In using the patterns of Psycho-Linguistics you are not going to randomly give suggestions to your subject. Rather, you are going to be putting him or her through processes which will build unconscious patterns to bring about the desired life change.

Sample Negotiation Steps

The first step involves setting up a way for you to communicate consciously; with the individual's conscious (aware) mind. This will be done in the following way.

1.   Set up *"yes"* and **"no"** responses. The easiest way is to lift each index finger in turn saying the words:

Move this finger for a *"yes"* and this finger for a **"no."**

2.   It is after setting up the conscious responses that you will begin to look for *unconscious response,* such as body jumps and movements concurrent with the conscious responses. When this develops you have access to the unconscious programs. Over the years I have found that receiving unconscious response is not quite as important as some NLP books would lead you to believe. With the use of hypnosis, by incorporating repetition and practice, the patterns will indeed become permanent.

Every client possesses the resources needed for change. If they didn't possess the abilities, the desire for change would not be present either. Most people are running old and inappropriate programs. Many have built such powerful beliefs around the behaviors of the past that they now are seeking the help of a therapist to access their own inner resources to effectively make positive changes in their lives.

The negotiation technique is used in all the patterns to come and is the therapist's mode of communication during the hypnotic state. If there is a part of the client that is resistant to change, it must be handled with understanding. That part of the psyche has a legitimate reason for holding on to the past. It is doing the best it knows how with the information at hand. When the new, more appropriate information is presented and the time is right for this change to be made, that part will be in full agreement. In fact, once that part discovers that the true underlying intention of the past can be met in more appropriate ways, the client will quickly and easily begin to display the new behaviors and attitudes. The mind is a success motivated servo-mechanism. It will always make the best possible choice with the information at hand.

We have all learned through the process of repetition. Our minds work with the information of the past to produce our reactions in the present. By use of the imagination our minds are able to store into our brain the new patterns as if they have been used often enough to become old dependable behaviors, thus changing the hierarchy of control to the new more appropriate behavior. The mind doesn't know the difference between real and imagined; it is all stored and categorized as information to be accessed and used.

Trance Management Methods

This section is designed to give you some examples of ways in which you can maintain the altered state for your clients or yourself.

1. **Realize that everything you say has the potential to either deepen the trance or to awaken the subject.**

   Example Suggestion: *Everything I say and every breath you take will guide you deeper and deeper into hypnosis.*

   All the information you gathered during the pre-talk is now your means of presenting the suggestions within your client's model of the world. If your client's lead system is *kinesthetic*, you are going to have to word your suggestions in a way that will allow him to *feel* them working in his life. This is true with the *visual* and *auditory* access as well. The *visual* person will need to *see* the suggestions working and the *auditory* person will need to *hear* the new suggestions involved. In addition, you will use *impact words* whenever possible.

2. **Set up a blue-print of the session.**

   Example Suggestion: *Whatever you need to see, hear or experience today, your unconscious mind will bring it to you.*

Remember to always go through the outcome questions before you put someone into the altered state. It is important that you know where you are going so you will know you are there when you arrive.

3. Set up a safe place.

Example Suggestion: *As you go deeper and deeper into relaxation you will become more aware of your mind. Negative thoughts and influences will have no control over you at this or any of the other levels of consciousness.*

Through the use of impact words, and with the person's outcome in mind, you will find this very easy to accomplish.

4. Give more than what your subject seeks.

Example Suggestion: *If there is any cell, any system or any organ of your being that is not working in perfect order for you, then that system, that cell, that organ will cease, it will stop, and begin to function in light and in love, just as it was intended the moment when you were born.*

During any session it is important that you point out to the client that the changes made today are stepping stones to an even better tomorrow.

5. Give each client a reason to awaken each day.

Example Suggestion: *Each day as you awaken, you begin to realize that it is the beginning of a new day . . . a bright new experience. You can begin to remember the moment you were born. You were given the opportunity of a lifetime with new eyes with which to see, new ears with which to hear and a body with which to function freely through life.*

Let your clients know that the moment of power is not in the past or the future, but NOW, and that as they take action in the present, their view of the past changes and acceptance of a better future becomes realized.

6. Give all clients positive statements when their body moves suddenly or makes unconscious response.

Example Suggestion: *That's right . . . you are doing perfectly.*

Each of your suggestions should support the effort of the unconscious mind. It is my belief that the conscious mind is like the laboratory or training ground for new behaviors. After the new behaviors and attitudes pass the test of the conscious mind, they are then sent back to the unconscious mind where these new patterns are generated when needed. Take the time to pace the conscious mind into the acceptance of the more appropriate patterns and behaviors.

7.   Set up a testable process that will allow your subject to know that he or she is in a state of hypnosis.

Example Suggestion: *Some people feel a lightness or a heaviness in their body, others feel a tingling sensation . . . whatever you are feeling is uniquely yours. No two people feel the same in a state of hypnosis . . . so move into that feeling and go deeper with each sound you hear around you.*

As stated earlier, in many ways hypnosis is a "conviction phenomena." Some test or proof needs to be given so that the person knows the changes have been made. With the ease by which the mind accepts the new programs by following the process of Psycho-Linguistics, the person could have made the change and be totally unaware of it. You will want to instill this awareness so that the client can go out into day-to-day activities convinced that changes have indeed taken place.

8.   Build a strong and resourceful anchor.

Example Suggestion: *Think of a time when you had the skills and abilities you would need for the future. Remember a time when you had confidence, pride in yourself and a positive attitude . . . breathe the way you were breathing . . . see through those eyes, hear through those ears, sense and feel with that body . . .*

A resourceful anchor is your "ace in the hole." If you keep a resourceful anchor within reach, you will always have the ability to guide the subject back to awakened consciousness in a positive state. It is important to guide your clients back to the fully awakened state seeing, feeling and hearing themselves positive and motivated.

The above suggestions are meant to be guides for you to follow as you develop your own style. Be aware of that style as you create your own trance management techniques. It is most important to follow your intuition, from a point of caring, and to let it be your guide.

"The thing always happens that you really believe in; and the belief in a thing makes it happen."

FRANK LLOYD WRIGHT

Hand Levitation During Trance Technique

This technique is written as if the subject has already been placed into a relaxed state. We have found that this is one of the best techniques to prove to the clients that they are in the hypnotic state.

. . . Now that you are relaxed, I want you to become aware of your hands . . . become aware of the hand that is lighter. I am now going to give a direct suggestion to your unconscious mind . . . Unconscious Mind, you are now going to make the hand which is lighter get lighter and lighter, but only as slowly as you can convince the conscious mind to relax the body . . . so the lighter the hand becomes the deeper the body will go into relaxation.

Your hand is getting lighter only as slowly as your unconscious mind can convince your conscious mind into relaxation. For the lighter the hand becomes, the deeper you will go. From this point on your hand will get lighter and lighter and begin to lift. It might start on your finger tips or perhaps your wrist. Just let it happen . . .(Repeat until the hand has lifted.)

Suggestion when the hands lifts: *Your unconscious mind will begin to show you the future . . . a bright and compelling future . . . a future where you have all that you need when you need it the most. Take all the time you need and slowly and progressively allow the hand to go down . . . only as slowly as you can believe and trust in a bright and compelling future.*

Suggestion when the hand returns to the lap: *You can begin to return back into the room, but only as slowly as you can awaken to look through new eyes, to hear through new ears, and to experience life in such a positive and powerful way that you will know that a change has occurred . . . and you can take a deep breath and return back into the room.*

Hand levitation can be used in many different ways and is an effective tool for letting the therapist know where the subject is within the trance state.

*"Courage is doing
what you're afraid to do.
There can be no courage
unless you're scared."*

EDDIE RICKENBACKER

Chapter Six

Dissociation Resource Technique

The purpose of the Dissociation Resource is twofold. First, most people seem to readily have answers to everyone else's problems but are unable to find solutions to their own. With the use of the Dissociation Resource the client will be able to look at his or her own problems as if they are happening to someone else. The other reason is that when someone is in a "stuck" state or a negative state he or she is not likely to make high quality decisions. Dissociating helps to move that person past the negative state and into at least a neutral state where a fresh choice can be made from a new perspective.

There is one client in particular who comes to mind in regard to the Dissociated Resource. This middle-aged woman, named "Alice," came to me with a very troubled past. She was unable to recall anything of her life prior to the age of thirteen. She knew that something from her childhood was troubling her, it seemed each day of her life, but she feared her past so much that she avoided allowing any childhood thoughts into awareness. In truth, she didn't know what caused such apprehension since it was completely hidden from her conscious knowledge.

The first step with Alice was relaxation to help her experience some release from her anxiety. I took her through a progressive relaxation and then began questioning her. Alice easily moved into a deep state of hypnosis. It seemed almost as if she had become suddenly eager to resolve what had troubled her for so long. In this state she began to relive the experience. Her voice tone and tempo changed and she became that thirteen-year-old girl again. Alice became distressed when she realized that something, she didn't know what, was about to happen.

I immediately had Alice become aware that she was in the room with me, relaxing and in a state of hypnosis, where she can now review the scene in her mind. I told her that it would be safe for her to go back to the time when she was thirteen, but this time as the adult that she is today. I then took her a step further away by having her imagine that everything occurring in that incident was, in fact, happening to someone else. Her unconscious mind could now play out the scenario as if it were happening to another person and not to her.

Alice was now able to view the scene with very little agitation and the shocking truth was revealed. At the age of thirteen Alice had been molested by an older neighborhood boy. This revelation brought many aspects of her behavior to light. Most notably, she now understood why she had always had a problem with men.

Alice was soon to be married for the third time. More than anything, she wanted this marriage to be different from the previous two. With a fresh perspective she began to see the pattern that had developed with all the men with whom she had been close. Once these relationships were established, she began to put up resistance and set up blocks to intimacy. Through the pattern of dissociation Alice was finally able to reveal the cause of her disharmony in relationships. With her newfound awareness she could meet the men of her life on a new foundation. Every man in her life was not this neighborhood boy, and they were not all out to hurt her.

When Alice first reviewed the event with the neighborhood boy, she described the situation with utter disbelief. Alice now needed to place that situation in a proper perspective within her mind. I had her go through the experience again, knowing that she was in the embrace of a safe and comfortable chair where she could make a mental review with the unique tool known as her mind. I instructed Alice that this incident could only be viewed from the mind of an adult, almost as if it were happening to someone else--only then would the unconscious mind be allowed to play out the truthful memory that had been hidden for so long.

Now, as an adult, Alice's past was set free. She began to recall other memories of her childhood -- memories that were positive, bright and compelling. All of these happy times from her life had been blocked by the one devastating experience. Once this incident had been uncovered, it was as if a very real weight had been lifted away. Interesting, because Alice's initial reason for coming to see me was because she was 75 pounds overweight. Alice found out that there was no longer any reason for her to carry the protection of the weight on her body. She was able to lift away the burdens and weight of the past by dissociating and unlocking the memories of her mind. If Alice had continued to try recalling the cause of the block without the Dissociation Resource, she may never have been able to uncover the true origin of her plight.

Her mind would have instantly brought up the old fears and brought up the safety shield that had always protected her from the memory.

Although the Dissociation Resource seems very simple in nature, I have found time and again that the ability to review the information from a new perspective can unlock the power and unleash the personal potential of each client. In fact, I use this technique often as a tool for my own problem-solving.

Guiding someone into the Dissociated Resource

1. **Set up** *"yes"* **and "no" responses.** You can do this in two ways, with either unconscious or conscious responses. The unconscious response is done outside of the subject's awareness, such as an involuntary muscle movement or an unconscious twitch. The conscious response, which I personally recommend, is simply set up by telling the subject, as you lift the index finger on one hand, that this is to be used for a "yes," and, as you lift the other finger, state that this finger will be used for a "no." *(Reference Negotiation Steps earlier in this chapter.)*

2. **Ask the subject to imagine that he or she is across the room looking back at his or her body over here.** Then place your hand on the anchor.

    EXAMPLE: *Take a moment to imagine that you are standing across the room looking back at yourself here in the chair. Take all the time you need. When you have done that please give me a "yes" response using your right index finger.*

3. **When the subject has this in mind, set the anchor by applying a little pressure.**[10]

---

[10]To set an anchor suggest: Become aware of what you are seeing, hearing and experiencing. Totally get into the state.

EXAMPLE: *Become aware of how you look from a distance. Notice your relaxed appearance. Notice the flow of each and every breath. Take a moment to relax and become aware of the dissociated state.*

4. **Break the state by having the subject open his or her eyes and look around the room.**

EXAMPLE: *Take a moment now to open your eyes and notice the lightness and darkness of the room. You are doing perfectly, remaining relaxed and comfortable with the process.*

5. **Ask the subject to think of a situation wherein he or she could benefit from looking at an experience from a new perspective.** Ask: *Where can you apply the resource in your life?*

EXAMPLE: *With your eyes open and relaxed take a moment to think of where in the future you could benefit from the power of dissociation. Think of situations where you could benefit from viewing your life from a detached perspective . . . a vantage point of power . . . knowing that from this perspective you are filled with many choices . . . some conscious . . . some unconscious. Become aware of how the mind processes information from this perspective. Knowing that the mind is learning new skills and new abilities that will help you to become more flexible and free.*

6. **When the situation is in mind have the subject close his or her eyes and guide through steps 2 and 3.** Trigger the anchor and ask the following questions *(elicit a "yes" response from the subject as each step is completed):*

EXAMPLES:

a. *What could you learn from this dissociated perspective?*

b. *How could you improve your reactions if you could dissociate whenever you needed to acquire a new view?*

    c.   *When could you use this resource in the next day, next week, next month to come to help you attain your outcomes?*

7.   Suggest that the subject can return to awareness of the room only as slowly as he or she can be convinced that there are now new and attainable solutions to problematical situations.

EXAMPLE: *As you become aware of the power of using your mind, and for a purpose, you can allow the unconscious mind to bring you fully back into the room only as slowly as all the changes that would need to occur can occur for allowing a smooth, effortless transition from the stuck states of the past to the new, flexible changes of the future . . . with a new perspective . . . a perspective that your unconscious mind will provide you . . . with a way and means to dissolve the feelings of fear, frustration, anxiety and depression so that upon awakening you can start an internal program of attaining your goals. Take a few deep breaths and take all the time you need to return to full awareness of the room.*

8.   Bring back to fully awakened consciousness.

"Nothing in life is to be feared.
It is only to be understood."

MARIE CURIE

Outline Dissociated Resource

1. Set up "yes" and "no" responses.
2. Ask the subject to imagine that he or she is across the room looking back at his or her body over here. Then place your hand on the anchor.
3. When the subject has this in mind, set the anchor by applying a little pressure.
4. Break the state by having the subject open his or her eyes and look around the room.
5. Ask the subject to think of a situation wherein he or she could benefit from looking at an experience from a new perspective.
6. When the situation is in mind have the subject close his or her eyes and guide through steps 2 and 3.
7. Suggest that the subject can return back into the room only as slowly as he or she can be convinced that there are now new and attainable solutions to problematical situations.
8. Bring back to fully awakened consciousness.

"A simple truth:
It's impossible to be depressed when you take action."

DR. ROBERT ANTHONY

Chapter Seven

Resource Organizer Technique

The Resource Organizer is a technique designed to utilize the power of the past, because that is exactly what everyone's past is -- POWERFUL. Can you imagine what your life would be like if you didn't have your past from which to access information? Without your past you would have to start from scratch every morning upon awakening, creating a new you with new thoughts, attitudes and beliefs. At times this might seem to be the best way, to lose memory of all your past blunders, but I assure you this would be more harmful than beneficial.

Besides, the mind doesn't store the information as it actually happened. In fact, it is stored in such a way that it is no longer true. We all change, delete, and distort our past. You will recall our two eye-witnesses to a single event with two totally different stories. These changes and distortions were probably not intentional, but, nonetheless, we are all guilty of this phenomena.

The distortions occur because our values and perceptions play a big part in the way we store information. It is not the purpose of this technique to change anyone's values or perceptions; these are key factors to any individual personality, although at times a shifting of perception can occur over time as the appropriate behaviors are used with a successful outcome.

With the Resource Organizer the client will review the information of the past and organize it, then re-file it in a more appropriate way, thus bringing about the desired outcome.

The past becomes beneficial simply by the individual beginning to think of it in a positive way. Almost every client that I have seen in my years of practice was positively motivated if the memories of the past were stored in color with movement and sound. So what happens if you have a negative event stored in techni-color and Dolby sound? The mind is then positively motivated to bring you more experiences of the same nature, which would ultimately be negative.

It has been my experience that people who are the happy-go-lucky type store any negative memories in black and white, or behind them so far gone that they can't recall them at all. They remember good times in color, surrounding themselves with the emotion of that experience and with loving positive sounds.

If the information of the past is stored in an appropriate way, the good times bright and alive and the negative events stored out of reach, then only the positive times will be brought up in future situations, resulting in higher quality decisions and, most importantly, a better overall state of mind.

I once worked with a client for alcohol addiction. He was a salesman named "Ken." He had always been a successful salesperson, but something had changed drastically in the last year. Ken's sales had dropped off tremendously. Now Ken sat before me, his head and shoulders slumped forward, his hands wringing, as he described what had happened over the last year. It was just about a year ago when Ken had experienced several successive failures which had begun to cloud his thinking. His usual motivation and determination had been lost. Clearly, a whole new cycle had taken over. Ken developed a new pattern which involved getting up in the morning, methodically going through the motions and plotting out his day's activities; but as soon as he would receive a few "no" responses, he would discontinue his efforts, procrastinate, get himself a drink and swear that tomorrow he would do better. He was swiftly progressing from a comfortable rut to a very uncomfortable one as pressure from his supervisor began to ensue and the effects of the alcohol took its toll.

Once Ken was in a relaxed state, I had him go back and review his memories of the past. At this point in Ken's life he was completely incapable of accessing that positive and motivated feeling of success. Before Ken went on a sales call, he had already seen himself failing. The failure syndrome was occurring continuously in his mind; all he had to do was play it out.

I pointed out to Ken that his customers were probably quick in picking up his unconscious cues and nonverbal communication and that, although he was unaware of it, he was probably selling a "no" response. Ken completely lost track of what he had always known. There are people out there who need his product, and who want to buy it from him. He had always known that sales was a numbers game; he simply needed to knock on enough doors to get enough "no" responses to finally get to the "yes." Ken knew that in sales, "no" means "yes." He had forgotten how to look at the "no's" from this proper perspective. Ken was now looking at those "no's" as a giant-sized wall that would require a great deal of effort to climb. Soon the walls were so overbearing and Ken was so tired that he didn't even notice when the *"yes"* response was within reach.

The first thing we needed to do was change the way Ken was accessing his information. I had Ken store every "no" behind him, as if it were money he was placing into his back pocket and ultimately taking him one step closer to a "yes."

I then took him through the process of mentally getting to "yes." I pointed out to Ken that what the mind views as mental practice, and what is actually done physically are all stored together within the unconscious mind. If each time Ken received a "no" response he mentally experienced three or four *"yes"* responses, his attitude would begin to change. The mind will take the medium between the two and give him at least a neutral and positive attitude going into the next sale.

Although it is true that some people are simply not cut out for the life of sales, Ken was, in fact, a superior salesperson. He had simply fallen into a rut of disbelief through repetitive practice and an anchor which he set mentally through his day-to-day activities; first by falling into commonplace activity and then by failing to set goals and accomplish them.

As Ken began to review the memories of his past, I had him take out that year of his life and reorganize it. Ken could now begin to view this time of his life as a learning experience. He had experienced a year wherein he had learned how to fail; and he did it very well. In fact, he did it so well that he would never have to repeat it.

At the completion of Ken's sessions he was able to go back to his career with the same attitude and enthusiasm that had brought him renowned success in his first years of sales. We found that with repeated practice of reorganizing his thoughts, he was once again on top of things, this time with a new ace up his sleeve, because he was now trained to use his unconscious mind to set up and accomplish goals.

As you read through the following technique to building a powerful past, remember that your past brought you to who you are today. So honor each and every experience, person, statement and dialogue that occurs within your mind. You can feel free to change anything to enhance the quality of your present day experience, because the past is only a memory, stored unconsciously, on the tapes of the mind. It is the present moment in which you can take action to accomplish your goals.

There will never be any power in blaming others for where you are or what you are going through. The power lies in taking action and changing what you can. *If you continue to think what you have always thought you will continue to get what you have always got.* The Resource Organizer builds new thoughts about the past which will, in turn, create new opportunities for the future.

Steps to Building a Resource Organizer:

1.   Have the subject close his or her eyes and set up *"yes"* and **"no"** responses.

2.   Get the subject to access a good feeling -- set up a Full Sensory Anchor. Ask:

    What are you seeing, hearing and experiencing? When the feelings are full within the experience give me a "yes" response. (At that point set the anchor.)

3.   Guide the subject back in time while holding the anchor.

    Example:

    Now that you have this feeling . . . you are going back in time . . . back to the earliest memory of this feeling. That's right, back to the very earliest memory, and when you are there let me know with a "yes" response.

4.   Once the past is accessed, ask the subject to notice how old he or she is in this time.

    Are you between the age of 0 and 5? 5 and 10? etc.

5.   Have the subject make a review of his or her past memories.
    Relax and imagine yourself moving through the memories of your past. Become aware of the good times of your life . . . stop and enjoy them for a moment . . . as you do, make the colors bright and brilliant to your mind . . . put all the love and emotion into each experience . . . feel free to put in even more love than you remember.

Place your favorite music in the background . . . just as if a Hollywood producer was playing a sound track to your life . . .

If an unhappy or negative memory comes up for you I would like you to take a snapshot of it . . . as if you are taking a picture with a black and white camera and the picture stops all the color, the sound is gone and the emotion dissipates as you now place each of the images behind you . . . One by one place all the negative experiences of your past behind you . . .

When you have done this once with the memories present within your mind today, just slowly open your eyes and return to full awareness of the room.

6.   Break the state, then reinforce the process.

Now that you have been through this process once, you can easily go through it again.   This time I want you to let me know when you are at the earliest unhappy or negative experience you can remember today.

Wait until you receive a *"yes"* response; suggest the following:

Take that negative time and place a large picture frame around it . . . like one you would see in a museum . . . When you have done that let me know . . .
Wait for *"yes"* response.
The picture at this time should be black and white.   If not, simply imagine that it is changing to black and white . . . in fact, from here the picture becomes so light and so bright that the images are gone.   You know that you had an experience in your past but it is no longer within view.   In fact, I want you to write on that blank canvas whatever you learned from the experience. That's right, I want you to imagine that you learned something positive from the experience of the past.   No matter how terrible it may have seemed in your past, see it now and into the future as a positive learning experience that will, from this day on, help you to avoid ever getting into a similar or worse situation in the future.

When you have completed that episode, move through the next experiences and then bring yourself back into the room when finished.

7. When the client has completed this process, discuss the past images. If needed, continue the above process until all negative experiences have been reorganized and stored in a positive way.

8. Once the changes have been made, bring the part of the past ahead to this time, then have the subject view the probable future with all the changes made.

How are these positive feelings going to benefit you in the future? Begin to see, hear and experience the future . . . all the positive changes that are going to occur for you in the next day, next week and next month to come . . . notice the benefits of changing the past.

9. Bring the subject back.

Only as slowly as you are willing to live in a powerful, positive state of consciousness do I want you to return to this room. Know that all you will need to do is think about the past and you will automatically go through this process making all the changes that will enhance your life experience today . . . Change the way the past is stored so that from this day forth you are building a bright and compelling future. Take all the time you need to return to full awareness of the room . . . the seconds are like hours, the hours are like days and the days seem to be weeks . . . all the time you need to convince your conscious mind that the changes you have made will occur before you open your eyes . . . and this is so.

"Optimist: a proponent of the doctrine that black is white."

AMBROSE BIERCE

Outline Resource Organizer:

1. Have the subject close his or her eyes and set up *"yes"* and **"no"** responses.

2. Get the subject to access a good feeling -- set up a Full Sensory Anchor. (At that point set the anchor.)

3. Guide the subject back in time while holding the anchor.

4. Once the past is accessed, ask the subject to notice how old he or she is in this time.   *Are you between the age of 0 and 5? 5 and 10?* etc.

5. Have the subject make a review of his or her past memories.

6. Break the state, then reinforce the process.

7. When the client has completed this process, discuss the past images.   If needed, continue the above process until all negative experiences have been reorganized and stored in a positive way.

8. Once the changes have been made, bring the part of the past ahead to this time, then have the subject view the probable future with all the changes made.

9. Bring the subject back.

"The optimist proclaims that we live in the best of all possible worlds; and the pessimist fears this is true."

JAMES BRANCH CABELL

*"Don't go around saying the world
owes you a living.
The world owes you nothing;
it was here first."*

MARK TWAIN

Chapter Eight

Compelling Future Technique

The Compelling Future Technique is used in all situations, with all techniques, and in every hypnotic session. People come to see a therapist because they want their future experiences to be better than what the past has brought them. In order for them to have a better future, they must first clarify what specifically they want to be better. They must know when, the times or instances, they want it to be better. And, most importantly, they must be able to imagine what that future will be like when it is better and all of the changes are in place. With a clear outcome, they can then readily create just how it will be achieved.

One of the fallacies of some therapies is that if you talk about a problem, analyze it, label it and try to make sense out of it, somehow it will eventually go away. It has been my experience that if you talk about a problem enough, you will soon get a "better" problem. An understood problem may be more sophisticated, but it is a problem all the same. The purpose of this technique is to program the future with the changes that are being made now. In NLP this is appropriately termed *future pacing*, which means to set up a program which will be triggered by a future event, thus ensuring success.

Future pacing is achieved by having the subject access the future in the way he or she would like it to be.

> *"What if the changes you wanted simply happened and you were in the future? What would you see, hear and experience that would convince you that a change has been made?"*

It has been my opportunity to work with many people who have achieved great success in business and in their lives. In one such experience, I was working with a rather successful millionaire in Scottsdale, Arizona, named "Frank." Now Frank had a rather unique problem. He had been able to make a million dollars three times in his life, but he was never able to hold on to the money.

During the process of hypnosis we found that, for Frank, there was a very real thrill in making a million dollars. But, once the money was made, his unconscious mind didn't know what to do, so he promptly learned how to lose it. This particular millionaire had gone bankrupt three times and made a comeback each time. Frank heard about my unique therapy process through a mutual friend and hoped that I would be able to remove whatever unconscious block was preventing him from maintaining his wealth.

After a few minutes of discussion with Frank I realized that he was living out what is known as a sabotaging belief system. Frank was indeed building a compelling future, but it consisted only of making a million dollars. Making the money was the goal he had placed unconsciously in his mind. He would promptly go about making the million dollars, and then just as promptly lose it, so that he could again gain a million dollars. If Frank had been able to maintain that pace he could have, in fact, been three million dollars richer at this time, rather than once again building up his million.

At the time Frank contacted me, he had a business plan in process which he knew was on the verge of bringing him his next million. We began a process of "upping the ante" by building an awareness of his future; that it holds more than money and more than a series of life events. Frank could now lift the limits from his perception of the future. That same thrill he experienced from making the money could be achieved by investing that million and making it ten million, or perhaps even one hundred million.

Frank began to see his compelling future in a new light. It is what would now allow him to awaken each morning with excitement and a readiness to go out and get what he wants from life. He realized that in the past, after each time he had made the million, he began to awaken each morning in a different way; he began to awaken with worrying and troubled thoughts about his money. He started making his investments with fear of losing and was making all of his business decisions from a different foundation than the one that had brought about success in making the money. Frank was setting up his own failure.

Through the Compelling Future technique Frank was able to set up other unconscious goals which could be met on a day-to-day experience. He began to organize his thoughts, attitudes and beliefs differently. It was no longer the "million" he was going after, but it was a life style; the ability to do all that he wanted to do, as he wanted to do it. It was this life style that compelled him each day to awaken with motivation and confidence.

The Compelling Future will work for any type of life enhancement. Sports improvement is another especially notable example. One way in which an athlete will be held back from performing his or her very best occurs when a coach doesn't allow the opportunity for displaying skills and abilities. When I was a freshman in high school, I was what they call a "wanna-be" -- I wanted to be something special, I just didn't know what. When I first started playing football, I used to tell people that I was a *"30-second wonder,"* with thirty seconds left in the game I would run out onto the field, get into my position, give a growl for defense, only to watch the quarterback snap the ball and fall on it, while we would all turn and watch the clock . . . 30, 29, 28 . . . until it went down to zero. I would walk off the field *wondering* why I had bothered to knock myself out all week in practice.

As I reflect on that time I realize what an impact my thought process had on my abilities. I had never even imagined myself in a starting position and I hadn't taken any action to improve my abilities. Somehow, I slowly made a transition on those thoughts. I began to run and work out everyday. I convinced my Dad that I just had to attend the State university's football camp, and so he let me earn the money to attend by painting the house that summer.

At the camp there was a coach who taught us about using the mind to achieve success. I remember his stories and suggestions clearly to this day. One day the coach brought in a place kicker to talk with the group about his successes in football. This kicker holds the record for the most consecutive place kicks in the University's football history. Here stood this great athlete before us, actually sharing his secrets to success. He said that before he ever kicked for an extra point, he would mentally see it going through the goal post and he would never lift his head to see if it went through until he knew that he had made the right connection. Being the son of a hypnotherapist, I was entranced by what I was hearing. These athletes were using hypnosis! They were setting up a bright and compelling future for themselves--they were seeing themselves in the future doing just what they wanted to do most.

The following year I attended another football camp. Here I had the opportunity to hear one of the greatest motivational speakers of our time--Bo Schembeckler. When Bo walked into the room everyone's ears perked and their eyes brightened as they listened to and watched this great leader. To this day I remember every detail of Bo leading us through a mental process of personal achievement. Whether or not he knew it, he was leading every one of us through a hypnotic process for goal programming. I remember later hearing the story of a lineman who, during the half-time of a football game, ran completely through the steel door that led to the playing field because he was so fired up and emotionally moved. He had just participated in one of Bo Schembeckler's half-time talks.

We can accomplish this same motivation with ourselves and, as therapists, for others. We simply need to know the right buttons to push, the appropriate future to perceive and the right words to say to ourselves or to others. Thoughts do indeed become actions, but it is a process. We must perceive a bright and compelling future before it can ever be achieved.

As you go through the steps to the Compelling Future, follow the mechanics of seeing, hearing and experiencing your future in the way you want it to occur. Then watch out and hold on--because our dreams will soon become reality. There is a statement that goes something like this: *"Life seems to go faster when you are living your dreams."* Become aware of the dreams that you are dreaming so that you can live what you want to live upon awakening.

To use the technique simply follow the steps below. These patterns are like templates for you to fill in with your own unique style and with the information that pertains to the individual client at hand. To be successful each therapist must be willing to be flexible with these patterns.

Steps to Creating a Compelling Future:

1. Set up *"yes"* and *"no"* responses.

2. Always use the **Resource Organizer** before using this technique.

3. Have the subject close his or her eyes and think of a future goal or outcome. Obtain a full sensory anchor. Ask:

   What do you see, hear and experience when thinking of that future outcome? What is your breathing like when you have that goal? Step into the image of yourself in the future. Become, for a moment in time, your future self.

4. Have the subject review the steps that led to the outcome but in reverse and noticing what events took place so that this outcome could become reality as quickly as possible. Give the suggestion:

   Take all the time you need to return back into this room. You can return only as slowly as you have reviewed the steps in reverse that will lead to the successful completion of your goal. Your eyes will open when you have returned to this moment and are back in this room.

5.   Break the state.

6.   Have the subject close his or her eyes once again and move through the next day, next week, next month to come and then to the day when the outcome has become a reality. Elicit a *"yes"* response when the subject has the day in mind, then re-anchor the state and bring the subject back into the room with positive feelings by making the following suggestions:

> *It is from this place that I would like you to review the next day of your life. As you move through this day let it lead you into the next week and the months to come. Know that each time you turn on a light switch you are turning on the new behaviors and attitudes that will bring about the successful completion of your goals. Each time you walk through a doorway you are walking through a higher door of consciousness that will allow you to make all the best decisions now and in the future. Take all the time you need to move through the days, the weeks, and the months to come, for the seconds are like hours and the hours are like days; and all the time you need to practice the new attitudes and behaviors is now occurring so that as early as today upon awakening you will move through life with a positive mental attitude of change. And this is so.*

7.   Continue with positive suggestions and bring the subject back into the room. Suggest:

> *You can return into the room only as slowly as you are convinced that all of this can and will become truth for you.*

> *"The only limit to our realization of tomorrow*
> *will be our doubts of today.*
> *Let us move forward*
> *with strong and active faith."*
> FRANKLIN DELANO ROOSEVELT

Outline For Creating a Compelling Future:

1. Set up *"yes"* and *"no"* responses.
2. Always use the **Resource Organizer** before using this technique.
3. Have the subject close his or her eyes and think of a future goal or outcome. Obtain a full sensory anchor.
4. Have the subject review the steps that lead to the outcome but in reverse and noticing what events took place so that this outcome could become reality as quickly as possible.
5. **Break the state.**
6. Have the subject close his or her eyes once again and move through the next day, next week, next month to come and then to the day when the outcome has become a reality. Elicit a *"yes"* response when the subject has the day in mind, then re-anchor the state and bring the subject back into the room with positive feelings.
7. Continue with positive suggestions and bring back into the room.

"They always say that time changes things,
but you actually have to change them yourself."

ANDY WARHOL

Chapter Nine

Resource Generator Technique

All individuals have inherent talents, skills and abilities which help to define their personality. The purpose of the *Resource Generator* is to take advantage of these unconscious actions by placing them into desired situations where they can bring about profound positive changes and enhancements.

As discussed earlier, we create our perception of reality through our values, beliefs and past programming. We also take for granted that what is true for one person is true for another, which is, of course, totally false in most cases. My meaning is quite simple. We all personally define reality through our own senses. Therefore, we have every right to redefine our actions so they become powerful and positive, helping us to reach our goals on a day-to-day basis.

Another way to explain this was told by my good friend, Gil. He tells the story of the three umpires, and it goes something like this:

> *There was a runner well on his way from first to second base. The throw was close, but as he reached the plate the umpire called him out. Another umpire, as he ran toward the plate, called the runner safe. And so the argument began. The home plate umpire watched this incident in silence and finally walked slowly out to second base to hear what was going on. After listening to the men in turn as they argued their case he promptly corrected them both, "This man is neither out nor safe until I say he is!"*

Thus is the story of life: it is neither good nor bad until you say it is. ꜛ ⁄

Unfortunately, reality doesn't come with clear-cut definitions. We form our opinions and shape our destinies with the information at hand. I ask you to think for a moment. What would happen if you could be in a positive state of mind all the time? What could you motivate yourself to do if you could, without conscious effort, simply take action and accomplish your goals? It doesn't matter what goal it is or how another perceives its importance.   What matters most is how you feel about its importance.

The best rule of thumb is to start simple and slowly build a trust in success that will follow you all the days of your life.   Nothing complements success better than the ability to change and modify old beliefs or outdated concepts.   Be prepared to soar like the eagles or contemplate like the owls -- whatever is needed at the time.   Flexibility at a time of frustration makes you a person in demand.

During a personal training session with one of the therapists, "Phillip," I asked him to think of something in particular he wanted to work on in his own life.   Phillip immediately spoke up and said "motivation!"   He explained, "It seems I put off those things I really want to accomplish in life. Even when I know that if I do them I could be far more successful than before."

I told Phillip not to worry because if he thought about it he would realize that most people are just like him.   They know exactly what to do, but don't know how to do it, or are afraid to access the change.

Phillip wanted to know why this occurs when they all know that the change will make their life better.   The truth is that they know, on some level, that once they make the change they will be unable to return to the comfort of the past--or what they are now perceiving as comfortable.   People would like to have some kind of generator to build resources for them, without any conscious effort.   I told Phillip that this is exactly what we are setting up with the Resource Generator.   We activate the mind to work out of the already working unconscious behaviors, but in new ways.

Phillip looked somewhat unconvinced so I explained further.   I told him that as he begins to work with clients he will usually take a moment before starting just to figure out exactly how to word his session for that individual's needs.   What if he could begin to think of all clients as an extension of himself? He can do this mentally because all clients will come to him out of a conscious belief that he can help them.   When you are working in the realm of the mind, there is no reason you can't be working on yourself at the same time.   I explained how, while doing a session with a client, it has often helped me to think that I was actually working on an unconscious part of myself; a part of which I was unaware until this person decided to pay me to work on myself! This one thought keeps me positive and motivated toward each new client. But, most importantly, it keeps me in a state of learning and understanding, and in tune with the therapeutic mind.   This has helped me time and again during therapy when those inevitable moments of frustration overcome me--I can suddenly become very flexible. If I could be as much like that person as possible, I could then ask myself, "What would I say to myself in this situation?" Invariably, I become able to deliver an unconscious dialogue that seems to fit his or her needs and beliefs.

I wouldn't say that this has worked 100% of the time, but if you find yourself in a "stuck" state, always remember that when you have prepared yourself, something positive will come of it. The mind works with intention. As long as your intention is to help, the message will come across as healthy and positive.

As Phillip sat in on my sessions during that week, he indeed began to notice that almost everyone, whether seeing me for insomnia, weight control, stopping alcohol or smoking, lacked the motivation to accomplish the change. One day toward the end of the week Phillip said to me, "I guess you're right; most people do lack the motivation."

I told Phillip he was almost right. In truth, these people didn't so much lack motivation, but were missing the desired outcome. They did indeed express a motivation--*one toward the old behavior*. The reason they lack motivation toward the new behavior is because their unconscious mind has not yet realized the benefits of the new behavior. The mind always works in the past and makes decisions out of repetition.

When the mind is making a choice, it will go deep inside to identify the responses of the past, then, using the *average* behavior, will feed out a response. When feeling on top of the world, you will usually respond to negative situations better than if you are feeling down. However, if you began to place the information and the resource into a generative mode--which means to contact something inside of you that happens repeatedly and link it to the new response--it will become like a friendly old habit. When it is linked in a positive way, it will be like a resource "generator" because the stimulus is already present; all you need to do is generate the new behaviors. If this process is done consciously at first, it will become an unconscious behavior rather quickly because the comfort of the old stimulus is built right in.

After he learned the Resource Generator, and went through the process himself, Phillip's motivation began to transform. He had been spending so much time motivated about procrastination that he became an expert at it. He was so motivated about putting things off that he had no motivation left to do the things he really wanted to get done. All Phillip needed was a change of focus and a shift in his thoughts; and then be prepared to succeed! For Phillip, as for most people, it wasn't a matter of success or failure. Rather, it was a matter of doing, and knowing that every moment in time is new and unique.

As you read through the Resource Generator, always remember that you are in power--that it's your life, your world and your day. So, today is a very wonderful day to make a change--it is the natural way of the universe.

Everything in the Universe is subject to change.
It is truly the nature of all things.
You are either going forward or backward; nothing stays the same.

Steps for Building the Resource Generator:

1. Set up *"yes"* and *"no"* responses.

2. With the eyes closed, have the subject think of a behavior he or she would like to display more often.

EXAMPLES: the ability to eat appropriately; the ability to be assertive; the ability to make a sound business decision; the ability to be relaxed and comfortable, etc. It can be any ability that he or she wants to possess.

3. Have the subject remember a time when displaying the desired behavior. If the subject is able to find a time go to step 5; if not, go to step 4.

4. Have the subject think of someone who has or displays the behaviors that will bring about the desired outcome.

    a. Once the person is in mind ask the subject to imagine watching this person go through one day of his or her life. (Make suggestions that the subject is learning to integrate the other person's attitudes and behaviors into his or her own mind.)

    b. After completing this person's day, ask the subject to imagine that he or she is inside this person's body; seeing through the eyes, hearing through the ears and sensing and feeling with the body of this person while moving through the day's experience.

c.   After step b, suggest to the subject:

Take the behaviors back into your own mind and imagine how you would utilize them in your future. What is it going to be like in the days, weeks and months to come when you have this new skill or ability and it is triggered unconsciously? At times this behavior will be there in your morning . . . at other times it will be there in your midday . . . and still at other times it will be there in your evening . . . but most importantly it will be there when you need it the most . . . that is in the days, weeks and months to come so that in a powerful new way you can experience your future. (Note: Reference Unlimited Reality technique.)

5.   Set a full sensory anchor. Ask the subject to remember what was seen, heard or experienced and allow that time to be real around him or her. At the peak of the experience gently press down on the back of the hand. (Remember the exact place where you set the anchor. For the process to work correctly you will need to touch the same place to get the same results.)

Suggest:

As you relax now begin to imagine seeing through your eyes, hearing through your ears and sensing and feeling with your body in a new way. What will the future be like for you?

Release the anchor.

6.   Ask the subject to now change this feeling to a color and then imagine filling his or her body with it. When subject is full of this feeling elicit a *"yes"* response. At that time anchor the state with a tactile anchor.

7.   Break the state by having the subject look around the room.

8.   Test the anchor. If the anchor is good, proceed with the technique. If you need to strengthen the anchor or add another resource, go back to step 2 and 3, whichever is needed.

9.   Ask the subject now to think of a time in the future when he or she would like the resource. When this is accessed, apply the tactile anchor, and then make it a complete sensory experience. Take the behavior into the future using the suggestion:

Move to the day when you are convinced that you have all the abilities you need to continue displaying the behaviors into the future.

10.   Bring the behavior back into the subject's reality and then bring him or her back into the room. Suggest:

As you begin to accept all the changes, beneficial behaviors and a fresh, new attitude, you can begin to return to full awareness of the room around you. But only as slowly as your conscious and unconscious mind can come to an agreement that the changes are positive, permanent and lasting through the rest of your life. Take all the time you need, and when your conscious mind is willing to use the resources of the unconscious mind on a day-to-day basis to improve the quality of your life, your eyes will open and you can return fully . . . wide awake and in perfect health.

11.   Make suggestions that the resource will occur unconsciously where needed in the future and guide the subject back to awakened consciousness. Suggest:

As you begin to sense the benefits of this new resource, you can contemplate the times in the future where it will work for you unconsciously and automatically . . . At times this new resource will help you in the morning as you look forward to a new day . . . a day full of successful events and a successful attitude. At other times this resource will be there during your midday helping you to handle the situations of the day in a positive and beneficial way . . . and at other times it will be there in your evening helping you to discover new ways to relax and enjoy your evening activities . . . finding yourself more relaxed around family and friends . . . But, most importantly, you will find a variety of new behaviors and attitudes when you need them the most . . . as you need them during your life experience... and this is so. You can return to the room only as slowly as you can be convinced that the changes have been made.

"Consider the postage stamp:
its usefulness consists in the ability
to stick to one thing till it gets there."

JOSH BILLINGS

Outline For the Resource Generator:

1. Set up *"yes"* and *"no"* responses.
2. With eyes closed, have the subject think of a behavior he or she would like to display more of the time.
3. Have the subject remember a time when displaying the desired behavior. If the subject is able to find a time go to step #5; if not, go to step #4.
4. Have the subject think of someone who has or displays the behaviors that will bring about the desired outcome.
   a. Once the person is in mind ask the subject to imagine watching this person go through one day of his or her life.
   b. After completing this person's day, ask the subject to imagine that he or she is inside this persons body.
   c. Take the behaviors back into your own mind and imagine how you would utilize them in your future.
5. Set a full sensory anchor. Ask the subject to remember what was seen, heard or experienced and allow that time to be real around him or her. At the peak of the experience gently press down on the back of the hand **Release the anchor.**
6. Ask the subject to now change this feeling to a color and then imagine filling his or her body with it. When full of this feeling elicit a *"yes"* response. At that time anchor the state with a tactile anchor.
7. Break the state by having the subject look around the room.
8. Test the anchor. If the anchor is good, proceed with the technique. If you need to strengthen the anchor or add another resource go back to step #2 and #3 whichever is needed.
9. Ask the subject to now think of a time in the future when he or she would like the resource. When this is accessed, apply the tactile anchor, and then make it a complete sensory experience. Take the behavior into the future.
10. Bring the behavior back into the subject's reality and then bring him or her back into the room.
11. Make suggestions that the resource will occur unconsciously where needed in the future and guide the subject back to awakened consciousness.

"First we form habits, then they form us.
Conquer your bad habits, or they'll eventually conquer you."
DR. ROB GILBERT

Chapter Ten

Unlimited Reality Technique

The Unlimited Reality technique is to be used when subjects don't feel that they possess the resources needed to accomplish the desired change or enhancement. Sports improvement and public speaking are two good examples.

It has often been said that we were all created equal. Well, if this was true, then we would all be just the same and the world would be a very boring place in which to live. NLP is, in one sense, a study of people and just what successful people do differently and consistently to get results that work. The Unlimited Reality Technique is the framework used to help one discover the attitudes and behaviors of another that he or she feels would be needed to attain the same or a better outcome.

This is my favorite technique to use with golfers. I usually start the session with one key question, "Can you think of a professional athlete who possesses the skills and abilities that you would like for yourself?" Most clients who are willing to pay a large sum to be hypnotized for improving their golf game know their sport pretty well and usually have at least two or three names immediately in mind. These clients come in with a jump on the program. They have watched and studied these desired athletes so many times that they already have appropriate mental tapes running in their minds; they just didn't know how to use them. The Unlimited Reality Technique is an excellent way to access those memories. With this technique the golfer in your chair can have a very real experience as the professional golfer he or she has watched on television. The next time your golfer views Jack Nicholas on television, he or she will no longer be an armchair official, but will be able to get into the game and be on the course, swinging the club with Jack. Whether training in golf, football, basketball or another sport, your clients can learn micro-muscle movements through a simple imaginative process, just as a child learns to walk and talk.

The bread and butter of a hypnotherapy practice is the client who wishes to stop smoking. When most smokers walk into a therapist's office they have no idea *how* they will be nonsmokers. I once worked with a subject named "Ellen," who had been smoking for over fifty years. Ellen was so convinced that she had no way out of her smoking behavior that she began to feel trapped within it. She had fully embraced the societal belief that it is difficult to become a non-smoker, that she has a physical addiction to nicotine and that she will gain weight as soon as she stops lighting up.

I started Ellen's session by reminding her that she was not born with a cigarette in her hand and was not placed in the smoking section of the nursery. Everyone is born a nonsmoker; it is a natural human state to be a nonsmoker.

I reminded her that as a child she learned by watching the people around her. Somehow, as a child, her eyes began to see, her ears began to hear, and her body began to feel based on what she was experiencing in the world around her. She would mimic sounds by listening intently and watching the source from which it came. She began to move her muscles just right so as to emulate that sound. I reminded her of how she learned to walk. I suggested that it may have happened something like this:

Ellen was lying in her crib on day and began noticing that everyone around her was walking around on two legs, while she remained on her back or belly, at best her hands and knees. After watching for a time she decided that if everyone else was doing it, she probably could too. She began to pull herself up, at first supporting herself on the side of the crib, and finding out that standing on her legs wasn't as easy as it looked from the world around her. The people who moved through her life seemed to do it with such ease. Soon, she became so curious that she just had to let go of the crib, but would invariably plop back down on her seat. At times the consistent falling may have even brought about an unconscious belief that she would never be able to do it.

But, something overcame that belief. Something inside of her told her that what others around her could do, she could also do, without question or hesitation. Ellen began to imagine herself walking like all the people she had been watching. She started out with crawling so she could build the strength in her legs and hips. She built strength in her arms so that later she could pull herself up next to a couch where she would feel the firm ground beneath her feet. Suddenly, after all her practice, the muscles would respond just perfectly and she would take a step, and then two. In no time Ellen was walking with ease, just as she had seen all the people around her do. She began to take walking across a room for granted. It can be accomplished without even a conscious thought and no effort at all.

I asked Ellen if she had ever noticed that a baby, once having learned to walk, will very rarely fall down again. She nodded her head acknowledging that she had three children of her own. Each of them, from the day they took their first steps, walked from that day on.

I told Ellen that this is the case with almost everything we learn to do in life. If Ellen could now tap into that learning resource within her mind, she could indeed learn to be a nonsmoker. Indeed, Ellen had tried to stop smoking on her own many times before. I explained that as humans, whether infants or adults, we learn through failure. But, a failure is never really a failure; it is only feedback. Our brain continues to feed us new information, upgrading that knowledge, as long as we don't accept it as truth until it works.

As I took Ellen through the Resource Organizer, she was able to imagine herself as a nonsmoker with whom she could identify. As she sat at her desk at work she would imagine herself as her boss, who found it very easy to walk through the offices without a cigarette. In fact, her boss had been a nonsmoker for as long as Ellen had known her. She found out later that her boss had, in fact, stopped smoking several years earlier.

Through this process Ellen discovered that nonsmokers do everything the same as a smoker, except they don't have the hassle, the worry, or the unconscious fear that cigarette smoking brings. She had lifted the burden of the past by activating the unlimited possibilities of her mind. There is a part of every one of us that absorbs new information and ideas through the experiences of others -- it is called curiosity.

Can you imagine yourself walking in another person's shoes? Can you imagine it with detail, including what is being said, heard, and experienced? What words are being spoken internally? Can you imagine the rhythm of that person's breathing. This is called micro-modeling and it is the foundation of the Unlimited Reality.

The **Unlimited Reality** technique is for those people who have no conscious concept of how they will act or respond with the desired change in place. I have even been known to send people out to rent a particular movie and watch it as if they are the character in the film, simply to get the experience from a different perspective. You may contrast this with the Dissociated Resource as the "associated resource," because you are going to fully associate yourself with another person's life and experiences, taking it on as your own, and remembering that the unconscious mind stores all information as truth, usable for future beneficial results.

Steps to Building an Unlimited Reality:

1.   Set up *"yes"* and *"no"* responses.

2.   With eyes closed, the subject thinks of someone who has the desired resource. Elicit a *"yes"* response when this access is made.

Suggest: *Close your eyes and think of someone who has a skill or an ability that you would like to develop . . . Take all the time you need . . . and when you have found such a person give me a "yes" response . . .*

Find out whether this person is male or female utilizing the *"yes"* and *"no"* responses. (For simplicity, I will use the male gender for this example.)

3.   Make the·suggestion that the subject is following behind this person watching him move through a day of his life. From a distance the subject is watching and noticing everything about this person. Have the subject give a *"yes"* response when the day is completed.

Now that you have found a person with a skill or an ability you would like to develop, I want you to follow behind him as if you are watching him from a distance . . . You can notice the look on his face, the movements of his body as if you are right behind him as he moves through his day displaying the behaviors that you desire . . . Take all the time you need . . . the seconds are like hours and the hours become days . . . and when he has completed the day displaying the behavior or attitude you desire give me a "yes" response . . .

4.   Now have the subject imagine the day again, this time from within the person's body. Give the suggestion:

Move through that day once again now but this time imagine that you are seeing through his eyes, hearing through his ears and feeling what his body senses and feels . . . You are just along for the ride . . . As if you can now understand his internal dialogue . . . what he says to himself while he is displaying this behavior or attitude . . . Take all the time you need and when you have made it through his day once again, let me know with a "yes" response. It's not necessary for you to see it, hear or feel it, just relax and imagine that it is all happening around you . . . you are doing perfectly.

5. Bring the new discovery back into the subject's reality so that he or she can benefit from the information on a personal level.

Now bring that experience into your own body and imagine using the resources that you have just experienced in your past . . . That's right, go back in time and reorganize your thoughts and feelings of the past looking through the eyes of change . . . hearing through the ears of discovery . . . and benefiting from the realization that what the mind can conceive and believe the body will naturally and normally achieve . . . Your thoughts become new things . . . your new concepts help to change and shape your perception of reality. Take the time to change your past . . . what changes have been made? How are these positive changes going to benefit you in the future when you need them the most? Take all the time you need . . . When you have completed making changes to the past, give a "yes" response.

6. Guide the subject into the future of his or her own life to discover where and when the resource could best be used.

Now that the changes have been established in your past, begin to think of things that will occur in your day-to-day activity that will trigger this resourceful new attitude. Think of the times and the places where you will benefit upon awakening . . . when you will be able to demonstrate a positive change . . . where a behavior of the past will be altered in such a positive and profound way that from this day forth you will constantly, on a day-to-day basis, make upgrades in your life experience. Some of the changes will happen in the morning upon awakening . . . helping you to feel fresh and alive . . . . ready to lead a successful day of discovering who you are by developing who you desire to become . . . Some of the changes will happen in and through your day as you look back over successful encounters where you simply made the right decisions at just the right time . . . You will find that as you enter into the deep stages of sleep your unconscious and powerful mind will begin to make a review of your day and in that review begin to make all changes and modifications that would need to be made so that in the days, weeks and months to come you will be in a constant positive progression of change . . . All the things that you do well will now be even better . . . with the use and power of your mind. What your mind can do for you is no small thing, but it is a big thing that can be done in a very easy way . . . So take a deep breath, relax and allow the positive processes of your mind to focus in on your future where you need the help the most . . . so that when you arrive the changes will already be made . . . Take all the time you need to see, hear and experience the future and when you are convinced that the changes have been made, and that your unconscious mind will provide you with all the necessary behaviors and attitudes to reach your goals, just give me a "yes" response . . .and then go ten times deeper into relaxation . . . And this is so . . .

7.   Continue steps 1 through 4 until the subject has built the unlimited reality needed to attain his or her outcomes. Ask the question:

Do you have all the resources you need to accomplish your goals?

You can use this technique both consciously and unconsciously. Your mind, that powerful resource which has always been there keeping you from harm, will remember this process so that in the days, weeks and months to come, if you come in contact with someone who displays a behavior or attitude that you would like to develop, even without your knowledge, you will simply begin to integrate the behaviors and attitudes that will help you to become ultra successful in all areas of your life . . . Take all the time you need to return to the room . . . You can return only as slowly as your conscious and unconscious mind can continue to communicate and develop a greater perspective so that every day in every way life can get better for you . . . and this is so. . .

Outline for Building an Unlimited Reality:

1. Set up *"yes"* and *"no"* responses.

2. With eyes closed, have the subject think of someone who has the desired resource. Elicit a *"yes"* response when this access is made.

3. Make the suggestion that the subject is following behind this person watching him move through a day of his life. From a distance the subject is watching and noticing everything about this person. Have the subject give a *"yes"* response when the day is completed.

4. Now have the subject imagine the day again, this time from within the person's body.

5. Bring the new discovery back into the subject's reality so that he or she can benefit from the information on a personal level.

6. Guide the subject into the future of his or her own life to discover where and when the resource could best be used.

7. Continue steps 1 through 4 until the subject has built the unlimited reality needed to attain his or her outcomes.

"The man who gets the most satisfactory results is not always the man with the most brilliant single mind, but rather the man who can best coordinate the brains and talents of his associates."

W. ALTON JONES

"Have you read anything by Stephen King?

How would you like to have his internal dialogue?

Not me!

For part of his motivation strategy he has a voice maybe two feet behind him that sounds like it comes from a deep subway. It roars, 'Get to work!'

This will keep you motivated.

RICHARD BANDLER
Time for a Change
Meta Publications

Chapter Eleven

Quantum Fusion Technique

The Quantum Fusion Technique is for that person who says, "I really want to change, but there is some *part* of me that just won't allow it to happen." The **Quantum Fusion** recognizes this "part" that seems to be holding on to past behaviors and attitudes. Once acknowledged it can then be "fused" with the part that strongly wants the change to occur. In reality, both parts are positive, or at least have underlying positive intentions. When the two are brought together they are much more powerful than either one standing alone.

Most addictions or problem states have a counterpart. For instance, if a middle-aged woman who has been smoking for 25 years comes into the office and says, "I really want to stop smoking but there is this part of me that really enjoys the taste of the cigarette." I will first explain that she may honestly enjoy smoking cigarettes, but it is more likely that she has trained herself to enjoy the taste and it started from a positive intention--not positive to her body, but positive to her mind. For most people, the first inhale from a cigarette was a horrible experience. Neophyte smokers will usually feel sick, dizzy and often cough or gag. But, somewhere along the line, they all "hypnotized" themselves to believe that it is an enjoyable experience. Remember, *the law of mind is the law of belief.*

The problem is not that these people don't have the skills and abilities to stop on their own. To the contrary, they have trained themselves to smoke and to enjoy it so well that they now need my assistance to stop. What they need more than anything is to stop focusing on the problem and begin to dwell on solutions. Sound simple? It is. Although hypnosis has been well known for helping people change quickly, I think the science of Neuro-Linguistic Programming has made it possible to guide another to a successful change almost immediately.

I have discovered that the Quantum Fusion technique is extremely powerful for almost every situation. I use it with virtually all of my clients at one point or another. Incredibly, it can be used either in hypnosis or just as effectively outside of a deep trance state.

I was once interviewing a potential hypnotherapist named "Judy." She was an honest and enthusiastic young woman of about thirty. I asked her whether she had used any form of mind technology for her own personal growth so that she could share her personal stories with others and also express conviction about the use and power of hypnosis. She told me that she had used hypnosis to lose weight and was now eating healthy foods and living a much improved life style. She then, rather sheepishly, admitted that she just couldn't seem to stop drinking coffee.

Since we were holding our meeting in a local restaurant, I asked Judy whether she would like to order a cup of coffee at that time. She acknowledged that, yes, she would very much like a cup of coffee. I summoned the waitress and soon Judy had a hot, steaming mug of fresh coffee before her and I had a cup of hot water for myself. As I took out my tea-bag (herbal from a health food store), I began to ask her certain outcome questions. I started by asking her just what life would be like for her if she was totally and completely coffee-free; what it would do for her. To my amazement, she began to describe, in detail, what her life would be once she was totally and completely caffeine-free. As she moved further along the story-line, getting lost in her new life, she also started slipping into a light trance state.

When she completed her story, I asked her, "What stops you from attaining this goal today?" She immediately began to tell me about "this part of me" that just couldn't seem to get anything done without the motivation and stimulation that caffeine brings. I stopped her here with a pattern-interrupt, by asking her to focus once again on her coffee.

I then placed my hands in front of me with the palms up. I explained that it was truly quite simple. "In one hand," I said, "there is a part of Judy who enjoys the taste, flavor and sensation of the coffee and caffeine. She acknowledged that this was correct. I turned one of my hands over and placed it on the table, then shifting my focus to the other hand. "And," I further explained, "there is another part of Judy who wants to be totally and completely caffeine-free," Judy was now nodding her head in agreement. "What are the positive benefits for Judy in being caffeine-free?"

She began to list them, one after the other. As she did, I made the impression that my hand was getting heavier, demonstrating that each time she listed a positive outcome it began to build a resource in my hand. She was soon watching the hand as she placed layer upon layer of resources in it.

I asked whether she could, just for a moment, step into that experience and live totally and completely caffeine-free. The moment that she was there I turned my hand over. I glanced at the art work above our booth and made mention of its beauty; breaking her state. I could then turn back to the hand holding the "negative resource" (the belief in the coffee), and said, "What does that part of you in the past really want?"

Instantly, without any hesitation, she said, "To get on with my life, to be motivated and to do those things in life that I truly want to accomplish."

I asked, "Is there anything stopping you from doing that, as early as today?"

She let out a laugh and said, "Well, I'm drinking coffee right now!"

It was now my turn to laugh as I pointed out, "Maybe you didn't notice, but you haven't even sipped your coffee since it was served."

As I picked up both hands, palms up, and slowly brought them together I began negotiating between the two, I said, "There is a part of you who wants this change to occur, and that part of you is functioning in the future, now. And, there is a part of you who perhaps wants this change to occur, but it is functioning in the past, then."

As I continued to bring them together I brought her to the conclusion that it is perfectly okay for the past convictions, beliefs or concepts to be slowly integrated in the future--the future now--which she will be living when she leaves this encounter. In truth, she doesn't have to make this change today. It can happen slowly. Some people simply discontinue drinking coffee on a certain morning upon awakening when they just feel good. There are mornings when you feel better than others, and it could, perhaps, be the day that would start a whole new life for Judy--the life she desired. I then gave her the opportunity to expand her success by adding that, by becoming completely and totally caffeine-free, it would prove to her mind that anything is possible--as long as she believes it possible.

I watched as she began to access the change and simply moved to other topics. As we broke up the interview I noticed that her coffee had sat and turned cold without ever being touched. As we parted I asked her to give me a call sometime the next day.

When she phoned the following afternoon, she asked about the interview and the position at our center. I told her that I wanted her to come into the office for some hands-on interviewing in which she would perform hypnosis with a client. As our telephone discussion progressed I sensed that there was something more she wanted to say, but she hesitated and I didn't push it.

Upon arriving at the office, she almost immediately blurted out that she hadn't had any coffee since our meeting at the restaurant. I smiled and told her I thought that was wonderful. I then asked her whether she thought she could make it through the rest of the day without the coffee. She shrugged her shoulders and stated that she really didn't think it would be a problem. I promptly took her into the future with that attitude by asking whether she thought she could go through not only today, but maybe a week. "Would one week be enough time for you to be totally caffeine-free?" She looked at me, a little puzzled for a moment, and then stated, "If I could make it three days it would be enough to convince me!" I told her that when she made it three days to give me a call.

Exactly three days later I walked into the office early and the phone was ringing. Before I could finish speaking Judy's excited voice came through the line announcing that she hadn't had any coffee for three days. In fact, she now is carrying herbal tea with her everywhere she goes so that she is prepared for any situation. I explained that it is the process of the unconscious mind to plan, prepare and generate results. She acknowledged that this was just what had occurred for her.

I knew Judy now had the conviction that would allow her to become a good therapist and she did indeed prove me right. After that, each time Judy and I went out to a restaurant together, we would both pull out our herbal tea bags and share a little laugh.

The main goal with most change technology is to get the subject to become congruent or unified in consciousness. As long as there is separation there will be unconscious stress. It is the purpose of this technique to bring a person together through a "fusion," so that all parts of the consciousness are striving for the best possible outcome for the whole.

Guidelines to Quantum Fusion:

1. Have the subject relax and place his or her hands in the lap with the palms up. Be sure that the hands are not touching each other. Have the subject close his or her eyes and think of an outcome.

Think of something that you would like to change about yourself . . . When you have done this let me know what it is . . . (You can also do this technique without knowing the subject matter. Just have him or her give you a nod of the head when the outcome is in mind.)

2.   Have the subject separate the polarities:

Go inside and find a memory of this behavior that you would like to change . . . And when you have it just nod your head so that I know . . .

3.   After the nod, reach over and anchor one hand. (This is easily accomplished by pressing into the palm of the hand with your thumb.) Suggest while anchoring:

Using your imagination think of the part of you that was responsible for this behavior in the past. You don't have to see, hear, or feel anything at all . . . just let your imagination go and find that part of you that was responsible for this behavior in your past . . . and if that part could become a color, any color at all, what color would it be . . .? Place that color in your hand.

4.   Once you have been told the color, break the state.

Now that you have a color in your mind I want you to open your eyes and look around the room knowing that each and every time I touch your hand in this way and ask you to remember the part of you in the past, you will remember all the feelings and sensations that go along with it . . . and this is so . . . Look around the room.

5.   With the subject's eyes closed once again, guide him or her back inside to find the part that wants to change.

Close your eyes once again and notice how relaxed you become by simply allowing your eyelids to feel heavy and to close down . . . It is from here that I want you to find that part of you that wants to change . . . it could be that part of you that functions in the future . . . the part of you that already knows the positive benefits of this change . . . take all the time you need . . . Remember, you are using your imagination . . . you don't need to see, hear or experience anything at all . . . just imagine it.   Imagine that this part of you could also be a color and that it could resonate in your other hand . . . when you have that color let me know with a nod of your head.

6.   Set an anchor of possibility. *(Press the palm of the other hand with your thumb.)* Suggest while anchoring the other hand:

Now that you have found that part of you that wants to make this positive change, and you are thinking of it as a color, you can begin to think of the possibilities . . . of what it would be like if you could access this part at will. Knowing that each time I touch you in this same place you will remember this color and the sensation of possibility . . . Fill your body up with this color as if you are an empty glass container . . . and when you are completely full, open your eyes and look around the room . . .

7.   Now comes the fusion process.

Close your eyes and become aware of my voice . . . allow it to resonate in a smooth and comfortable way between the right and the left hemisphere of your brain. Be comfortable and relaxed as you begin to think of the possibility in change.

8.   Reach over and fire both anchors at the same time. (Press your thumb into the palm of both hands at exactly the same time.) Suggesting:

What would it be like if the part of you that knows all the changes in the future could go back in time and retrain and modify the past . . .? (Pause)

What would it be like if the positive intention of the past could be met in new and different ways that would be just as immediate and appropriate? (Pause)

How would you know, through the days, weeks and months to come, that this has occurred . . .?

9.   Let go of the anchors. Suggesting:

Begin to think of the possibilities . . . if these two parts could somehow come together and help you to accomplish this goal. Using your imagination, begin to think of your hands . . .

How, in the one hand, you have this part of the past . . . which in the past did the very best that it could with the information at hand . . . it now and forever has access to new information . . .

And, in the other hand, you have this part of you that has a list of possible new behaviors and attitudes . . . a part that would be willing to provide these new thoughts and ideas as needed so that in the weeks and months to come you could make this change permanent and positive for the rest of your life . . .

Now, by using your imagination, let the hands slowly come together . . . but only as slowly as your conscious and unconscious mind are willing to work in a harmonious and balanced way to attain your goal . . . Take all the time you need to develop communication between the past and the future in your mind. As the hands slowly come together, there is a bonding that is taking place . . . It is such a powerful and positive bond that each and every time the hands touch together, either consciously or unconsciously, a change will occur . . . It will be a positive and profound change. I am not sure just where or when that change will occur, but your unconscious mind knows exactly where and when it would do you the most good . . . so slowly allow your hands to come together. You can take all the time you need . . . the seconds are like hours and the hours are like days. You have all the time you need . . . Begin to think of the new color that is created as the two become one new positive resource.

10.   When the hands touch together suggest:

Through the use and power of your mind the past and future have come together to help you attain your goals . . . and now fill your body with that new color. Imagine your body like an empty glass container . . . your body fills with this new color . . . your personal color of power . . . so that when you see this color in your world it will remind you of the decisions that were made here today . . . the decision to live life in a state of harmony, peace and abundance . . . knowing that all behaviors are positively motivated . . . and as your mind thinks of the positive results of this process other things begin to change . . . some of them will be conscious and you will realize that a change has occurred . . . Most will be unconscious . . . you will simply be making positive and beneficial changes with no conscious effort at all. The motivation and desire will be generated unconsciously . . . and this is so . . .

You can begin to slowly return into the room . . . but only as slowly as you can imagine the days, the weeks and the months to come . . . and when you come to that day in the future when you are convinced that all the changes have been made and that every day in every way your life is improving, then you can open your eyes and return to full awareness of the room around you, saying to yourself wide awake, wide awake . . . take all the time you need . . .

*"The weak can never forgive.
Forgiveness is the attribute of the strong."*

MAHATMA GANDHI

Outline For Quantum Fusion:

1. Have the subject relax and place his or her hands in the lap with the palms up.

2. Have the subject separate the polarities:

3. After the nod, reach over and anchor one hand.

4. Once you have been told the color, break the state.

5. With the eyes closed once again, guide him or her back inside to find the part that wants to change.

6. Set an anchor of possibility.

7. *Now comes the fusion process.*

8. Reach over and fire both anchors at the same time.

9. **Let go of the anchors.** Suggesting: *Begin to think of the possibilities . . . if these two parts could somehow come together and help you to accomplish this goal . . .*

10. When the **hands touch together suggest**: *Through the use and power of your mind the past and future have come together to help you attain your goals . . .*

"You will never "find" time for anything. If you want time you must make it."
Charles Buxton

CHAPTER TWELVE

Mind Link Technique

Although **Quantum Fusion** is one technique that you will probably use more frequently than any other, at times it is not appropriate to fuse resources together but rather to link them to each other. Advertisers do this all the time and quite effectively.

How do you spell relief?

If you said **R-O-L-A-I-D-S**, then your mind linked the Rolaids commercial with relief. The advertiser's intention was to take a negative state, such as intestinal upset, and link it with their product . . . *relief.*

The Mind Link technique places the individual into control of his or her "state." It has been my experience that all successful people have one ability in common--they know how to manage their states. Avoiding frustration is not the key. Rather, it is turning that frustration into flexibility; fear into power; anxiety into expectancy, and so forth.

The Mind Link is very effective for depression. People in a state of depression seem to fit a universal mold. Their shoulders are rolled forward and the head is down. This is where they are accessing feelings. You could also call it a state of "compression," because they are going deep inside for an answer, where they know a solution is at hand. By anchoring these people from the depressed state into one of possibilities, their mind will instantly move from the state of depression to one of expectancy or perhaps even excitement.

I sometimes smile as I look back to recall one of my first meetings with two women who had asked me to write a program for the DUI offenders in their state. They liked what I had to say, but they wanted me to prove that my techniques would work in the real world. They had shared a knowing glance, grinned and nodded, then gazed back at me. They knew who the perfect candidate would be. Her name was "Marcia," a young woman of 19 years who lived in a near perpetual state of depression. They said that if I was able to help Marcia, I certainly had something that could help the world. I was up for the challenge, so I asked them to bring Marcia in.

Before I move on with Marcia's story I would like to make clear that those people in severe states of depression should always be advised to see a medical doctor. I was informed that Marcia had been thoroughly examined and had no physical causes for her depression.

The first thing I noticed was that Marcia's neurology was certainly that of the typically depressed. I asked her what was happening with her life. Her statements immediately told me that she had developed a dim and distant view of her future. She had nothing bright and compelling in her future that might have otherwise motivated her. But, it would be impractical to attempt building a future from a depressed state. I knew that the only way Marcia would experience results was if she could be moved from the depressed state into a positive one where she could remain active and functional in life. The more she could move into the positive and uplifting state, the more she would accomplish and the further she could move from the negative states of the past.

I began to train Marcia's mind to move from one state to another. I asked her to get into the depressed state and as soon as she had the feelings I asked her to look up to the ceiling and think of three things she thoroughly enjoys doing; activities which have nothing to do with her present situation.

As Marcia looked up to the ceiling a smile crossed her face, and she began to feel better, without knowing why. Her physiology had begun a transformation. Her shoulders went back, her head was up — she was beginning to look further down the road of life. As soon as I recognized those signs of feeling good, I had her step into each of those situations and live them to the best of her ability. Then, as I broke the state, I noticed that she was sinking back into depression, just as she had trained her body to do. I immediately took her back up to the ceiling with three new situations — this time in the future. Her eyes rolled up and instantly the lips curved into a smile and a look of health and vitality began to appear. It's a proven fact that when you think healthy and positive thoughts, your brain will release endorphins which will naturally allow you to feel good. Once she went through these three future situations, I broke the state again.

As she looked around the room, I had her settle back in, and then turned to the two women to make a few comments. In these few moments I noticed that Marcia was sliding back into the depressed state once again, but this time it was to a much lesser degree. Once again, I had her roll her eyes up, this time throwing her shoulders back, and she began to play the game — the one of excitement.

Marcia was realizing that going after things in life can become exciting. Planning and promoting success internally can feel like magic. It becomes a form of addiction — a positive addiction — which can improve the quality of everyday life. And the best part — it could all be set up just as you would program a computer, so that it happens automatically upon awakening in the morning.

I told Marcia that her mind works perfectly, and that instantly and automatically her mind could remember just what it was like when she rolled her eyes up to the ceiling. I wasn't sure how often she would need to do this process, but she knew. She promptly told me that if she did it three more times she would be pretty well convinced that it would work forever. I told her to go ahead and take herself through the same process three times, and when she was finished to let us know.

As we were deep into conversation about our future plans, Marcia's cheery voice suddenly broke in. "I'm done," she chirped. We all smiled at her and continued about our business. Marcia sat and listened attentively. Her body remained erect and her eyes bright. Marcia had changed her thinking process simply by changing her body's posture. She had been able to link her mind to new experiences.

When I saw Marcia again only a week later, she was quick to point out how exciting and positive her life had become since she had learned how to use her mind to instantly imagine what she wanted. She was now able to realize how, in the past, she had actually placed herself into the depressed state. She described how, after the first few days of practice, she began to change her states automatically, without even knowing what was happening. I told her that her unconscious mind could continue this process and it would soon slide into an unconscious behavior completely outside of her conscious awareness.

Marcia had previously shown little motivation toward a career. She had bounced from job to job, each new position lasting only a week or two before she would quit or get herself fired. However, Marcia had built her own future where she is now successfully running her own business as a manicurist. She is frequently heard expounding on the merits of excitement and challenge in her work. She thoroughly enjoys being her own boss and making her own choices.

There are many situations where the Mind Link can come into play. Depression, stress, frustration or anger are the emotions that best respond to this technique. These are the states when a person feels out of control, with no excitement or movement toward goals. There is nothing worse than being stuck in a state and not knowing how to get out of it.

Steps to Using The Mind Link Technique

Follow the simple guideline below and transform failure states into powerful new triggers that will boost creativity and productivity.

1. Set up **"yes"** and **"no"** responses using the index fingers.

2. Have the subject think of an unwanted state. (Examples: anger, fear, frustration, anxiety.) Suggest:

Go inside and think of a state in which you feel "stuck," such as fear, frustration or anxiety, and when you have that give me a "yes" response. Think of the state you would most like to change.

3. Get a full sensory anchor. Take the subject back to the earliest memory of this feeling. (Touch the back of the hand.) Suggest while anchoring:

Now that you have a state that you would like to transform, begin to realize that you trained yourself to have this response . . . you now have the ability to learn a new response. Go inside and let your mind drift and wander back in time to the earliest memory that you can recall today of experiencing the unwanted state . . . and when you have found that earliest memory let me know with a "yes" response. It could be a memory as a child or it could be a memory of something that occurred as early as today. Move to that early memory and when you are there let me know . . .

4. Break the state.

Take a moment to notice that each time I touch you in this way you will remember this time and all of these feelings. And now you can open your eyes and look around the room . . . Take a deep breath and look around the room . . . That's right . . .

5. Ask the subject to think of the opposite of the unwanted state or feeling.

Take a moment now and think of what the opposite feeling or state would be . . . Think of a time in your life when you were in that opposite state . . . Fully get into this state . . . What were you seeing? What were you hearing? What feelings did you experience? Imagine that you are there now. What would it be like . . .? Give me a "yes" response when you have done this . . .

6. Get a full sensory anchor in a different place. *(Touch the shoulder or opposite hand.)* Suggest while anchoring in a different place:

And now begin to realize that each and every time I touch you in this place you will immediately begin to think of the positive and beneficial resource . . . Remember the way colors look in your mind when everything seems to work perfectly . . . Remember what you say to yourself . . . Recall those wonderful positive feelings . . . let them fill your body . . . It's perfectly okay to feel good and accomplish your goals . . . When your body is full of these feelings you can open your eyes and look around the room . . . (Let go of the anchor when the eyes open.)

7. Access the unwanted state (hold for at least 5 to 10 seconds) then trigger the opposite anchor and make the suggestion:

What would it be like if the next time you began to feel this (the unwanted state*) you immediately felt this* (the opposite state)?

Roll your eyes up as if you are looking up at three doorways . . . Each doorway has an opposite feeling and behavior from those of the past . . . these are positive new behaviors from which you can benefit as early as today . . . When you have this in your imagination give me a "yes" response . . .

8. Once you receive a **"yes"** response. Suggest while touching the positive anchor:

Imagine that you are going through doorway number one . . . and instantly and automatically you begin to display a new behavior different from the behaviors of the past . . . Allow yourself to view this without question . . .

stepping into the experience, seeing through the eyes of change, hearing through the ears of change and sensing and feeling with your body as if you were actually in the future displaying this new behavior . . . And when you are done give me a "yes" response . . . (Release the anchor.)

9.   Once you receive a **"yes"** response continue. Suggest:

Step back out of doorway number one and step into doorway number two . . . (Press down again on the positive anchor) *. . . Again, begin to fully experience this new behavior noticing how well this behavior could work in the future . . . Take all the time you need and when you are done give me a "yes" response and step back out of doorway number two . . .* (Release the anchor.)

10.   After the **"yes"** response guide the subject through option number three. Suggest while touching the positive anchor:

You have already been through two options that you could use to discover your outcome . . . so now step into door number three . . . Make this a behavior that you would perhaps never imagine yourself doing . . . Make this behavior even a little ridiculous and fun . . . This third door will be the door of flexibility . . . If there is a behavior between door one and three that might be appropriate in a situation, the unconscious mind will provide it upon awakening so move through this last doorway . . . See through your eyes of the future, hear through your ears, and sense and feel what your body would be feeling if you were to experience this state upon awakening in the future. Take all the time you need and when you have done this let me know with a "yes" response . . . (Let go of the anchor.)

11.   Putting it all together.

Now that you have seen, heard and experienced three new behaviors begin to think once again of the unwanted state of the past . . . (Touch the anchor for the unwanted state while suggesting*) . . . This is the past that you are wanting to transform into a positive and resourceful state . . . And when you have that state give me a "yes" response . . .*

12.   After getting a **"yes"** proceed by letting go of the unwanted anchor and touching the desired anchor and suggesting:

Once again, what would it be like if the old feelings instantly and automatically brought about these new options . . . where you would instantly walk into each doorway and then decide which one would be best for you at that time. Begin to think of three different situations in the future where this would be beneficial . . . (Pause)

Now, in your mind, move in and through each door discovering which behavior would be best for you and when you find that behavior say to yourself. "Yes, I will do that." . . . And then think of three places in the future where you would want to display this behavior unconsciously . . . where the unwanted state could instantly be transformed into a positive new resource state. Take all the time you need and when that has occurred bring your awareness back into the room and open your eyes so that I know . . . (Release the anchor.)

13.   Testing the process.

Ask the Question: *When you think of the undesired state what is it like now?*

Watch the eyes — if they roll up to visual construct from a feeling than there is a strong possibility the new patterns have been successfully installed. If not, continue to take the subject through step ten until you can notice a definite state change, eye roll or both.

Remember that the purpose of this technique is to guide your subjects from a stuck or undesired state to a positive or suitable state where they will be able to make a different and more appropriate choice in behaviors or attitudes.

Outline for Mind Link Technique

1. Set up **"yes"** and **"no"** responses using the index fingers.
2. Have the subject think of an unwanted state
3. Get a full sensory anchor. Take the subject back to the earliest memory of this feeling. (Touch the back of the hand.)
4. Break the state.
5. Ask the subject to think of the opposite of the unwanted state or feeling.
6. Get a full sensory anchor in a different place. (Touch the shoulder or opposite hand.)
7. Access the unwanted state (hold for at least 5 to 10 seconds) then trigger the opposite anchor and make the suggestion: *What would it be like if the next time you began to feel this* (the unwanted state*) you immediately felt this* (the opposite state)? *Roll your eyes up as if you are looking up at three doorways . . . Each doorway has an opposite feeling and behavior from those of the past . . . these are positive new behaviors from which you can benefit as early as today . . . When you have this in your imagination give me a "yes" response . . .*
8. Once you receive a **"yes"** response. Suggest: *Imagine that you are going through doorway number one . . .* (Release the anchor.)
9. Once you receive a **"yes"** response continue. Suggest: *Step back out of doorway number one and step into doorway number two . . .*
10. After the **"yes"** response guide the subject through option number three. Suggest while touching the positive anchor: *You have already been through two options that you could use to discover your outcome . . . so now step into door number three . . .*
11. Putting it all together. *Now that you have seen, heard and experienced three new behaviors begin to think once again of the unwanted state of the past . . .*
12. After getting a **"yes"** proceed by letting go of the unwanted anchor and touching the desired anchor and suggesting: *Once again, ...*
13. Testing the process. Ask the Question: *When you think of the undesired state what is it like now?*

> *"All men should try to learn before they die
> what they are running from, and to, and why."*
> **JAMES THURBER**

CHAPTER THIRTEEN

Quick Phobia Release Technique

The Quick Phobia technique was developed by the founders of NLP. This technique has undergone many modifications since its creation. It has been my experience that, even though the founders of the original technique claim to do the process in seven minutes or less, it truly depends upon the subject. This is probably one of the best techniques to display the genuine effects of NLP to instantly modify and improve a person's behaviors permanently. I have used this process on over a hundred clients and have found that in every case the subject experienced a beneficial change. Although, unlike most NLP practitioners, I also guided the client through hypnotic techniques to reinforce the new skills and abilities. I am not certain that this is necessary, but since I am in a referral business I want to make sure the change is permanent. Also unlike other professionals in this field, we guarantee success with most of our programs.

When I first started in the field of hypnotherapy, I had a group get together at my house every Tuesday night to discuss the latest mind techniques and processes. On one particular evening, after guiding the group through what I perceived as a pleasant hypnotic experience, I noticed that one person, "Thelma," looked very upset and puzzled. When I finally asked her what had occurred to make her so upset, she started crying with deep, racking sobs, which was quite unnerving to the group. I allowed Thelma to continue to cry as I went around the class and discussed each of their experiences. I then asked the class to go on break. They all took the cue and went to another room.

I was now able to ask Thelma about what had happened to so thoroughly upset her. Thelma told me that she had a snake phobia and that during the hypnotic session, for some reason unknown to her. she had imagined herself being attacked by snakes. She could think of nothing that would have prompted this mental image, but it was clear that it had upset her greatly.

Fortunately, at this same time I was in the NLP training process and had just learned the Quick Phobia Release. I knew that this technique could work for Thelma, but I would have to be flexible in using it since she was in such a state of agitation. I took her through the process and found out that as she released the synesthesia (reaction) of the mind to the pictures, the image and the internal stimuli, she was creating a distorted and far worse impression in her mind than reality could ever be. In her imagination she had been bitten by innumerable snakes before she had ever seen one.

After I took her through the Quick Phobia technique, Thelma was able to return to the class with a smile and the reflection of a new inner peacefulness. She was feeling wonderful and positive — much to the disbelief of the others in the room, for just minutes ago she had been crying and seemed quite miserable. Now she appeared rested, relaxed and confident. Indeed, the group was puzzled, but no one spoke up at the time.

At the next week's meeting Thelma explained to the group that when she had gone home a week ago it was the first time she was able to walk through her home without the fear that snakes were slithering across her floor, a nightmare with which she had lived since childhood. She said that she felt more free, confident and peaceful than ever before.

Another example of how the Quick Phobia can work came when I was doing a hypnosis demonstration for a friend at a local event she was sponsoring. There were a variety of demonstrations and lectures going at the time, and so some local television and radio people got together and decided they were going to do a show proving that hypnosis wasn't real. I was scheduled to do one of my stage demonstrations in which I put a few subjects into the hypnotic state and have some fun.

As I walked through the crowd after my show, a woman stopped me. She had read my biography and taken note that I was an NLP practitioner. Her purpose in intercepting me was to inform me that "that NLP stuff doesn't work." I responded with, "What do you mean it doesn't work? Everyone works perfectly!" I further explained that NLP is the "science of people" and its intent is to help people to improve themselves and their lives. I then asked her how she had come to such an uncompromising conclusion about NLP. She explained that she had gone to an NLP professional (one for whom I had great respect and trust), who had taken her through the phobia technique and it had failed completely.

I asked her to stay for awhile, until I completed some business, so I could discuss her experiences further. I told her that I would like the opportunity to show her just how well NLP would work right there in the night club. Jane's husband had been listening in on the conversation and as I turned to walk away he handed me a plastic spider and told me to try throwing it on her sweater and I would see the immense phobic reaction it would create. I knew that, for the phobia release to work, there must be a true phobic reaction.

This technique will indeed work for fear based realities as well, but it would need to be done in a slightly different way.

Later, when I returned to Jane, I said "Hello," and, as I reached out to shake her hand, flipped the spider onto her sweater. Sure enough, she had an incredible reaction. I don't think she appreciated my action much, especially when her husband was standing nearby roaring with laughter.

I guided Jane through the Phobia Release technique. But because her reaction had been so strong, I didn't let it end there. After she had been through it once, I asked her whether this was the same method as the other NLP practitioner had used. Her reply came with a sly, "Yes." I now knew for certain that I would have to do something *more* and *different* to convince her conscious mind that it would work this time.

I told her we were now going to do something a little more diverse. Since she had done it once, and then done it again, she could now split the screens in her mind so she was seeing the situation in two separate places. As I took her through the process, I noticed her eyes accessing the memories, on the split screens, and she started to show signs of relief. The phobic situation was beginning to have less and less of an impact. With these signs of success I was able to continue the process until she had so many screens of time, encountering so many different spiders, that in her unconscious mind she had probably met every spider that could possibly enter her life experience from that moment on. At the time when I finished the process she seemed somewhat confused, so I went about my business and made a point to see her later, with my friend the plastic spider.

When I threw the spider at her this time, she caught it and looked at it, then stated that she knew it was plastic. I reminded her that she knew it was plastic before, but it hadn't stopped her from reacting. I reinforced the new behavior by telling her that I would give her a call a week later to find out how well it was working, and she could tell me about all the marvelous results she had in life by overcoming this one phobia.

Since that encounter we have become friends. Jane is very gifted with mental abilities herself and we found out that the Phobia Release had in fact worked for her—even when done in a night club with hundreds of people, noise, commotion, and the media present.

To become truly proficient with this or any of the Psycho-Linguistic patterns you will need to be flexible within the process. Most of your subjects will have little or no knowledge about hypnosis, NLP or the techniques you are using. You are the expert! Just as I changed the technique to fit Jane's needs, you too can make alterations to fit the needs of your varied clientele.

Your first step will be to discover whether your subject is accessing a true phobia or is simply living out a fear-based reality. First of all, it is imperative that you notice the reaction, or the negative anchor. Some therapists even keep rubber snakes, spiders and other paraphernalia of common phobic reactions. What is most important is that you, as a therapist, have a concrete concept of what that phobic reaction is for your client. One way to inspire a phobic reaction is by the simple mention of the word. In a true phobia the person will begin to tremble, the face will flush, or you may be presented with a look of absolute horror. The best test is to simply bring up a situation wherein the reaction has occurred in the past. Then watch closely. If it is a true phobia there will be a noticeable change in the physiology.

Steps to Using the Quick Phobia Release

1.   Access the phobic state. (Test to verify the fact that what you are dealing with is truly a phobia. This process will also work on fear, anxiety, depression or any other unconsciously motivated behavior, but time has proven that this technique works best for phobias.)

When was the last time you experienced the phobic reaction? (Get a full sensory anchor.) *Go inside and then describe to me what you were seeing and hearing . . . What did your body feel like? . . .* (At the peek of the experience set a tactile anchor.)

2.   Have the subject dissociate and think of all the possible positive reasons for having this phobia. Discuss how this phobia perhaps is protecting him or her in some way. Review the ecological reasons for the phobic reaction of the past.

Return your awareness to the room . . . Now let's think of this phobia in a new and different way . . . Let's assume that this behavior is motivated by a positive intention . . . that something positive is trying to be expressed deep within you . . . Because you had this phobic reaction in the past, in what positive way could it be working for you? . . . Perhaps keeping you from harm or helping you to learn? . . . Use your creative mind to think of all the possibilities . . . possibilities that are positive. It does not matter whether the underlying reason is true or not . . . just allow your creative mind to think of a list of positive reasons for the past behavior . . . Remember that whatever the real positive intention is, it will always be met . . . only now and in the future it will find a positive and beneficial outlet . . . one that will allow you the freedom from the past phobic reaction . . . Take all the time you need to discover the positive underlying intention . . . And when you have it let me know so that we can continue this session . . .

3.　　Set up **"Yes"** and **"No"** responses and elicit responses after each step.

Close your eyes and become aware of my voice . . . allow my voice to become smooth and comfortable for you . . . It is from here that with each and every word that I utter and each and every breath that you take, you will go into a peaceful, positive place for change . . . So with that, I want you to use this finger for a "yes" (reach over and lift one of the index fingers) *. . . relax and go deeper and deeper to that perfect state of relaxation for you . . . Now I want you to use this finger for a "no"* (lift the index finger on the other hand) *. . . And go deeper and deeper with each and every response . . .*

4.　　With the eyes closed have the subject imagine himself or herself in a theater, comfortable and relaxed.

Now that you are becoming more and more comfortable, I want you to imagine the inside of a theater. It could be a theater that you have visited, or one that you are just now making up for the purpose of this session . . . it really doesn't matter . . . When you have created this theater in your mind, give me a "yes" response so that I know, and we can continue this process . . .

5.　　Have the subject imagine a black and white snapshot of himself or herself on the movie screen before the phobic reaction starts. (It could be a time in the past or a time in the future.)

Imagine now that the curtain is being drawn back and on the scene is a black and white picture of you . . . this is a black and white picture of you before the phobic reaction starts. You are sitting back in one of the seats in the theater watching the scene over there . . . And in that scene there is a black and white picture of you before the phobic reaction starts . . . it could be a past or future time. When you have this image in your mind give me a "yes" response. . .

6. Now have the subject imagine that while sitting and watching the picture on the screen, in a still picture, that he or she floats out of the body in the chair and into the projection booth.

As you imagine yourself watching the black and white image of you on the screen . . . you begin to float out of your body sitting in the chair and you float up to the projection booth where you can now imagine watching yourself down in the chair, watching yourself on the screen, in a still frame snap shot in black and white. You will stay in the projection booth until you are given the suggestion to leave . . .

It is from here, as you look down out of the projection booth, that you can see yourself, where you are watching yourself on the screen, and begin to think of all the skills and abilities you will need in the future to overcome this old behavior. When you have made a mental list of all the behaviors and attitudes you would need, give me a "yes" response and go deeper and deeper.

7. Have the subject imagine that the black and white image is coming to life so that the new behaviors and attitudes will be sequentially programmed for success.

You are now watching yourself watch yourself, and you will stay in the projection booth as the black and white snapshot begins to turn into a movie. This is not just any movie, this is a movie about you moving through the phobic reactions of the past . . . The movie can begin now in black and white . . . As you watch yourself down in the seat, you are in the movie theater watching yourself on the screen, going through the experience of the past . . . And when you have made it successfully through the experience give me a "yes" response so that I know . . .

8. When the subject gives you the "yes" response have him or her jump from the projection booth into the scene and have it fill with color.

As you have now made it through the experience imagine yourself jumping from the projection booth into the image on the screen . . . Now take a deep breath of relief and begin to color the picture. Place sounds around you and experience those wonderful feelings of knowing that you have made it . . . Fill yourself with the emotion of that experience. Like an empty glass container fill your body up with these positive emotions . . . And when you have done this and have the feelings of making it, give me a "yes" response . . .

9.   Get a full sensory anchor and have the subject imagine that all the images, sounds and feelings are going quickly in reverse while bringing up the feelings of knowing that he or she is going to make it. When the subject is back at the time before the phobic reaction starts have the subject give you a **"yes"** response. Suggest as you reach over and set the anchor:

Now imagine that you are going back through time. Imagine that all the scenes and all the sounds are running in reverse . . . That's right . . . everything you remember occurring during and after the phobic reaction of the past . . . I want you to imagine that everything is going in reverse . . . and when you are back at the time before the reaction of the past was triggered open your eyes and return back into the room (release the anchor) . . .

10.   When the subject returns into the room test the process by suggesting:

Now when you think about the phobic reaction of the past what occurs?

Note: Calibrate the difference in the response.

11.   Find out how many times the subject feels that he or she would need to go through this process so that it will work unconsciously as early as today.

Because you have been through the process once, you can remember the steps and now see yourself in the scene, in black and white, before the reaction of the past . . . Watch yourself float up out of your body and into the projection booth. When you are in the projection booth start the film. When you get to the point in the scene where you know that you have done it . . . when you know that you have taken all the steps to protect yourself and have kept yourself from harm, just jump into the scene . . . Feel the emotions of knowing that you have made it . . . fill yourself up like a glass container . . . then move back through time in reverse as fast as you can, faster than before . . . And when you have done that again NOW . . . open your eyes and return fully back into the room . . . here and now, where the positive underlying intention has been modified . . . in such a powerful and positive new way that this new behavior will be where you need it the most, just as you need it . . . and this is so . . . (pause). Take all the time you need . . . But before you open your eyes think of three places in the future where you could benefit from using this technique . . .

12.   Ask the subject to go through the process five times on his or her own and let you know when it is completed.

Because we have done this once . . . and you have reviewed this process once again . . . you have really done this process twice, and again just NOW . . . So now go back through the process five times and watch yourself with the new resources . . . opening your eyes and looking around the room between each process. Remember to run the process in full color in reverse as fast as you can . . . When you have done the process five times, let me know with a "yes" response . . .

13.   Once this process is completed break the state again. Ask:

Are you sure you have done the process five times? . . .

Note: The subject should go up and review the process five times to make sure that it has, in fact, been accomplished.

14.   Ask the subject what it is now like when he or she imagines the phobic reaction of the past. If you witness any phobic reaction, have the subject do the process three more times. If it appears that the reaction has been appropriately changed, you are done. Continue to step 15.

15.   Have the subject practice and future pace.

When is the next time you will be in a situation to test this process in the future? . . .

Allow the subject to give you a response, then suggest:

What is the future going to be like now that you have this new resource at work for you? Close your eyes and imagine the days, weeks and months to come and just how nice it is going to be now that you have this new skill and ability . . .

I say to you now . . . every night as you drift off into a dreamy drowsy state of sleep your superconscious mind is going to take this information into your dreams . . . As you begin a sequence of dreams that will bring about the success of your life and this program, you will sleep deeply and rhythmically, knowing that your mind, and what it can do for you, is no small thing, but it is a big thing, that can work for you in a very easy way . . .

I say to you now . . . you will begin to dream of all the possibilities . . . of everything that could or would occur in your future . . . and this time begin to think of just how this new process is going to fit in unconsciously so that you will be unaware that it is even occurring . . . in the same way that you are unaware of the part of you that is presently beating your heart or controlling your breathing . . . this new process has already gone back through time . . . through the memories of your past . . . changes have already been made . . . powerful and positive changes that will simply work for you in the days, weeks and months to come . . . changes that will convince you that every day and in every way life is getting better for you . . . and this is so . . .

Take all the time you need to integrate this new behavior so that instantly and automatically through the rest of your life it will be there keeping you from harm . . . Take all the time you need to move to the day when you're convinced that all of this is working for you . . . When this has occurred, open your eyes and return into the room . . . take all the time you need . . . the seconds are like hours . . . the hours become days . . . and the days flow into weeks . . . take all the time you need NOW to return into the room . . .

*"Nothing in life is to be feared.
It is only to be understood."*

MARIE CURIE

Outline for Quick Phobia Release

1. Access the phobic state.
2. Have the subject dissociate and think of all the possible positive reasons for having this phobia.
3. Set up **"Yes"** and **"No"** responses and elicit responses after each step.
4. With the eyes closed have the subject imagine himself or herself in a theater, comfortable and relaxed.
5. Have the subject imagine a black and white snapshot of himself or herself on the movie screen before the phobic reaction starts.
6. Now have the subject imagine that while sitting and watching the picture on the screen, in a still picture, that he or she floats out of the body in the chair and into the projection booth.
7. Have the subject imagine that the black and white image is coming to life so that the new behaviors and attitudes will be sequentially programmed for success.
8. When the subject gives you the **"yes"** response have him or her jump from the projection booth into the scene and have it fill with color.
9. Get a full sensory anchor and have the subject imagine that all the images, sounds and feelings are going quickly in reverse while bringing up the feelings of knowing that he or she is going to make it. When the subject is back at the time before the phobic reaction starts have the subject give you a **"yes"** response. Make reinforcing suggestions as you reach over and set the anchor.
10. When the subject returns into the room test the process.
11. Find out how many times the subject feels that he or she would need to go through this process so that it will work unconsciously as early as today.
12. Ask the subject to go through the process five times on his or her own and let you know when it is completed.
13. Once this process is completed break the state again.
14. Ask the subject what it is now like when he or she imagines the phobic reaction of the past. If you witness any phobic reaction, have the subject do the process three more times. If it appears that the reaction has been appropriately changed, you are done. Continue to step 15.
15. Have the subject practice and future pace.

"I've got to keep breathing.
It'll be my worst business mistake if I don't."

SIR NATHAN MEYER ROTHSCHILD

CHAPTER FOURTEEN

Producing Analgesia: Glove Anesthesia

Hypnotic suggestion earned its foundation in the medical and scientific arenas through its demonstrated effectiveness in surgery. In the mid to late 1800's surgical knowledge was advancing throughout the medical community. However, most people risked undergoing an operation only when they were convinced that death was the only alternative. Why? Imagine yourself undergoing an operation while fully conscious and sensitive, probably with several attendants holding down your arms and legs!

It was during this time that Dr. Esdaile, a British surgeon practicing in India, decided to try hypnosis as a means of pain control during the surgical session. In the first year he was not completely successful, but later he perfected his technique and performed most of his operations without any disturbance on the part of his patients.

What Dr. Esdaile discovered was the body's analgesia, our own natural anesthesia. Chances are good that surgery under hypnosis would have grown as a science were it not for the development of chemical anesthesia.

There are many purposes for today's hypnotists to produce hypnotic anesthesia for their clients. One such use is to help a subject who has a fear of the dentist, which is, in truth, a fear of the potential pain involved. Or, a subject who is allergic to the chemical anesthesia may find hypnosis a welcome alternative. Pain-free childbirth is another use; and the list goes on.

In proportion to the results achieved, the technique seems almost unbelievably simple.

"Never a lip is curved with pain
That can't be kissed into smiles again."

BRET HARTE

Steps for Using Glove Anesthesia

1.   Ask the subject to close his or her eyes and imagine the eyes cannot open at all.

Notice that your eye muscles and tendons are going loose, limp and totally relaxed. In fact, so loose, so limp and so totally relaxed that you won't be able to open them at all. Just imagine in your mind's eye that they are like rubber bands lying on a table top, loose, limp and totally relaxed. Concentrate your attention now on your eye muscles and tendons . . . and notice that they won't open at all . . . and when they are that relaxed, just try to open them.

After the subject has tried to open them, move to number 2.

2.   Suggest:

Now that you are relaxed I'm going to have you count in reverse from 100 to 0 and every number is going to take you deeper than the number before . . . When you reach the number 97, all other numbers will drop from your mind, drop from your thoughts and drop from your awareness.

3.   Start the counting process:

Client: *100*
You: *Deeper and deeper, the numbers are dropping.*

Client: *99*
You: *Deeper and deeper, the numbers are dropping.*

Client: *98*
You: *Deeper now . . . as the numbers are dropping.*

Client: 97
You: *Let the numbers go now . . . out of your mind and out of your thoughts.*

4.   After client has lost the numbers suggest:

I'm going to move your hand and when I do, I will drop it back into your lap. Let it fall loose, limp and completely relaxed . . . just like a wet dish rag . . . loose, limp and relaxed . . . completely and totally relaxing.

Continue to drop the hand into the lap until the hand and arm drop loose and limp like a wet dish rag.

5.   Choose one of the subject's hands and state that you are going to apply a little pressure. As you apply the pressure with a very slight pinch, ask the person if the pressure is being felt. When it is acknowledged let up on the pressure. Move on to "a."

    a.   Stroke the back of the other hand suggesting:

Numb and anaesthetized . . . going completely and totally numb and anaesthetized. (Continue stroking the hand and repeating this suggestion.)

    b.   After a few moments, tell the subject that you are once again going to apply a little pressure. Pinch the hand that you anesthetized hard enough to leave marks. Apply a small amount of pressure to the other hand. While doing each hand state:

A little pressure, let me know when you feel a little pressure.

6.   Count the subject out:

1 . . . 2 . . . 3. . . , eyes open . . . look around the room. Notice the marks on your hand.

After you have applied the pressure to both hands and pinched the one hand leaving a mark, count the subject up to awakened consciousness. Have your subject notice the marks on the hand that was pinched. Chances are your client will express a great deal of surprise since he or she probably felt only a light pressure. Your client can now be quite easily convinced that the same analgesia that allowed only the feeling of pressure as you applied the marks can also be used for whatever purpose your client has chosen; whether you are guiding him or her into a state for painless dentistry or to a surgical situation without anesthesia.

Again, there are a multitude of deepening techniques, and this is only the pre-testing process for producing glove anesthesia. After you have done the test and have confirmed the subject's ability to create glove anesthesia, then the appropriate hypnosis session is to be applied. This way the client can be guided into a state of total numbness and anesthetization throughout the entire body. In a situation where the process is being used for a medical or dental procedure, the process should be performed under a physician's supervision.

Outline For Glove Anesthesia

1. Ask the subject to close his or her eyes and imagine the eyes cannot open at all.
2. Make suggestions for the subject to count backwards from 100.
3. Start the counting process.
4. After client has lost the numbers suggest: *I'm going to move your hand and when I do, I will drop it back into your lap. Let it fall loose, limp and completely relaxed . . . like a wet dish rag . . .*
5. Choose one of the subject's hands and state that you are going to apply a little pressure. As you apply the pressure with a very slight pinch, ask the person if the pressure is being felt. When it is acknowledged let up on the pressure. Move on to "a."
   a. Stroke the back of the other hand suggesting: *Numb and anaesthetized . . . going completely and totally numb and anaesthetized.*
   b. Pinch the hand that you anesthetized hard enough to leave marks. Apply a small amount of pressure to the other hand.
6. Count the subject out: *1 . . . 2 . . . 3 . . . , Notice the marks on your hand.*

"My creed is that: Happiness is the only good.
The place to be happy is here.
The time to be happy is now.
The way to be happy is to make others so."

ROBERT INGERSOLL

Chapter Fifteen

Psycho-Linguistics and You

It is my belief and conclusion that Psycho-Linguistics, NLP and hypnosis are the new frontier of psychology. We are living in a fast paced, high-tech society -- one that wants fast change. Nightingale Conant and other book and tape manufacturers make a billion dollar business out of motivating people through positive thinking and self-awareness. Now, too, it is becoming a major part of psychology. I believe that those in the people-helping professions will quickly find that the archaic methods of personal encounters in the psychological setting will be left behind as the demand for quick change increases. The processes of non-contextual therapy as has been defined and demonstrated herein will become the therapy of choice.

Neuro-Linguistic Programming, which is the foundation of Psycho-Linguistics, has proven itself effective over the past fifteen years and is now considered the front runner in new technology that stimulates the mind and accelerates the change process.

People are becoming more and more aware of the benefits involved in imagery, hypnosis, Neuro-Linguistic Programming, meditation, prayer and positive thinking. More and better modalities for personal change are being developed every day, lending credibility to the field as a whole and bringing about a more rapid healing for the planet. I am convinced that the work I am doing, along with thousands of other therapists and trainers, is a catalyst to the evolutionary shift of humankind. I am pleased that you have chosen to join us.

The dialogue that follows is for you as therapist. It is designed to help you create the mind-set for using the psycho-linguistic patterns. You can record this transcript onto a cassette tape and, using the power of your own voice, give yourself a preparatory mind treatment before going into a session.

ALIGNING WITH THE THERAPEUTIC MIND

*Quiet the mind and focus deep, deep inside. Focus on your breathing by noticing how one set of muscles is breathing in . . . and the lungs themselves respond by naturally releasing out. So it is with the mind . . . You are able to listen to your clients and allow the intuitive mind to invent the session that would be most appropriate for each individual client to experience. You are utilizing all the skills of the **therapeutic mind** to monitor the breathing of the client. You will naturally notice how the subject breathes in . . . and breathes out. Then you can notice how your breathing coincides with that of your client.*

*And . . . naturally . . . you will notice the **eye accessing cues** . . . How when the eyes roll upward the subject is accessing **visual** information . . . and when the eyes roll from side to side, the client is accessing **auditory** pieces of information . . . and when the eyes roll downward, you will know that **kinesthetic** information is being processed. And . . . naturally . . . you are always willing to **calibrate** and test these assumptions because you know that the process of therapy is one of **pacing and leading** . . . leading your clients in the direction of their goals.*

During each session, you will discover how your mind can become clear and focused. Each session is a new session . . . and the therapeutic sessions of the past are now resources that will help you to build the constructive future that you desire.

Once again take in a deep breath . . . and notice how this deep breath helps cleanse the body all the way down to the bottom of the feet . . . and the feet and ankles go loose, limp and completely relaxed. Now, feel the grounding of information from all books that you have read, all seminars you have attended, all positive pieces of information that could possibly help you to use your intuitive, therapeutic connection to create a session that is most appropriate for the client at hand. Notice the power of relaxation flowing through you. Perhaps you are now beginning to recognize how everything that happens through you must also happen to you. Therefore, each suggestion is positively stated in the affirmative.

Now you may be noticing how the calves and shins are relaxing . . . so relaxed and comfortable that flexibility moves into the knees. You are flexible and open to the possibility that through you today, a process or technique that may have never before been spoken, could be, and perhaps will be, spoken through you. Open your mind to the possibility in guiding your clients through whatever "stuck state" in which they may find themselves, and to the accomplishment of their goals.

Trust that you will recognize your clients' **outcomes** and selectively hear their **impact words** as you ask the questions: What would you like? Where would you like it? How often would you need to display the new behavior, and with whom? Both consciously and unconsciously you will remember to check the **ecology** in each idea or concept . . . and your **negotiation skills** are naturally improving. You will be noticing both conscious and unconscious cues that will allow you the consistency you desire for your session. Each time you enter into a therapy session, to create the optimum communication possible, you will notice that your body will remain relaxed and comfortable. You will be guiding your client through the **pacing** and **leading** process into such a deeply relaxed, positive state that outside sounds and influences will only prompt you to remain more focused on the task at hand. You will allow the information to flow to you and through you.

Now you may want to notice how the thighs and hips are relaxing. Concentrate, using your mind's eye, on how the client will walk in and how comfortable you will feel in greeting your client. Notice how you will be able to use all the **rapport skills** you have built over time . . . and how your rapport skills are getting better and better. In meeting your client you remain comfortable and relaxed and you feel confident in each word that you speak. Your rapport skills are so fine tuned that your body **matches** and **mirrors** in exactly the right sequence, tone and tempo for you . . . you are doing perfectly. You are getting the taste of therapy and noticing the smell of success. In your mind's eye, concentrate on how you will lead your clients from confusion into a state of focus and balance.

You will find yourself naturally **future pacing** each technique as the days become weeks . . . and the weeks become months . . . and the months become years. You will continuously scan the situation to notice all **visual cues** . . . all **auditory cues** . . . and all **kinesthetic cues** that will help you to provide the information necessary to complete the therapeutic sequence. Each time you enter into a therapy session, your quality will improve . . . your ability to produce results will improve . . . and as you mentally imagine your subject in the relaxed and natural altered state, you will notice that as the subject's eyes close down, and with a few deep breaths, you will guide your client deeper into a positive and productive state known as hypnosis. Your skills with **hypnotic language patterns** will improve . . . you will notice the flow of each word and with every new session the words will flow more consistently in the direction of a deeply relaxed and positive state.

In a moment my voice is going to pause. During this quiet time, I ask that you imagine the complete session taking place. You may choose to use the **Quantum Fusion** *technique, where the part of the past and the part of the future merge together to create the dynamic moment known as now. Perhaps you will choose to use the* **Mind Link** *technique to link resourceful positive states into less-than-positive behavior patterns. Allow your mind to focus on the possibilities of double* **dissociating** *in the* **Quick Phobia Release** *as you watch yourself over there on a screen of space . . . watching yourself relaxed and comfortable and noticing that all skills, abilities and resources you need will flow to you and through you as you need them the most during the session. I don't know exactly which of the techniques you will need to use today . . . but you do . . .*

As you move through the process . . . simply take a few deep breaths and scan your body . . . notice how you are keeping the positive thoughts resonating through your body as the hands and the arms relax . . . the chest, abdomen, back, neck and head area all relax. When you have completed the sequence of how your client will be guided through the hypnotic process with the eyes remaining closed and comfortable . . . and you have successfully guided your client through all the procedures that will bring about success . . . then notice how your client leaves your office . . . Notice how positively your client has responded . . . and how positive you feel. You know that you did the very best you could given the information you had available. From here you will take the time to review over the session and create all other probabilities for success so that each session will improve upon those you performed in the past.

I'm now going to pause so that you will have all the time you need to finish the sequence of thoughts that will structure a positive and resourceful session and bring about the results your client desires . . . Then, and only then, will your eyes open . . . at that point you can return to the room and full conscious awareness.

The next transcript is for you to use at the completion of your sessions so that you are always "upgrading" the "program" in your therapeutic mind. It will also be beneficial in clearing the mind of any negative feedback that may have been a part of the session. This guided imagery should also be recorded in your own voice. You may wish to record one tape with your pre-session process on one side and this post-session process on the other. Each will help you to assess your therapeutic approach and keep your mental battery on full charge.

RE-CHARGING THE THERAPEUTIC MIND

Take in a deep breath . . . and let that breath out with a sigh. Notice the calm between the right, creative side of your brain and the left, analytical side of your brain. Notice the way in which your mind and your body are creating a cleansing from within by using each new breath now.

Breathe in the color of white . . . breathe it in and mentally wash from your mind all thoughts, ideas and concepts about the session. Become neutral with every piece of information that was shared . . . whether the information was positive or negative, just let it go. By mentally recharging the body you can become neutral to the experience. As you breathe in deeply, once again, mentally recognize how you can make a deep, meaningful connection with the therapeutic mind. Whatever you will need to see, hear or experience to learn from the session you just administered or from any prior encounter, will naturally flow into your awareness . . . and at just the right time.

Notice how the facial muscles and tendons respond to the positive suggestions to relax now. Feel how the relaxation moves into the face and flows back into the scalp. As the scalp relaxes, you may be noticing just how productive your body can feel in a deeply altered state of relaxation. This soothed and comfortable response can then move down through the neck and shoulders . . . lifting the weight of these past experiences from your shoulders. Whatever you said during that session . . . whatever you experienced and whatever you perceived as your client's experience . . . imagine the new possibilities now awakening in your mind as you use that positive information for yourself. Imagine what type of connection you might have had with that person . . . What possible purpose could you have had when drawing that individual into your experience? Was it to create a clearing for yourself? Perhaps to make your own positive changes right along with your client?

In your mind's eye, notice how everyone to whom you are associated is somehow connected with you through beliefs, habits or patterns. Notice how you are helping others to develop an awareness of their full potential, thus increasing your own awareness and ability to use your potential. Activate your inner ability to imagine that you are relaxing comfortably in the same position in which your client rested and relaxed. Can you imagine the possibility of using each positive suggestion for yourself? Imagine the way the arms to the fingertips will respond upon awakening if each positive suggestion could be applied in your personal life. Whether or not you have the same "problem" as your client is irrelevant . . . is it not? Imagine that your mind could take you deep, deep inside to select out a behavior, attitude or belief that could change or improve through the use of the suggestions given to you by your client's experience . . . because you have already discovered how all that happens through you must happen to you . . . have you not?

Notice how the mental energy flows down through the chest, abdomen and back . . . clearing your body of the experience . . . and allowing you the empowerment necessary for handling each new client with resourceful skills that will only get better. As you allow the days to become weeks . . . and the weeks to become months . . . you can mentally imagine the many ways in which this session could have been different. After you have reviewed the session once in your mind, I want you to review it once again but using different techniques and suggestions. Perhaps you will discover a body movement that was consistent, but of which you were previously unaware. Once again you can notice the tone and tempo of the client's language patterns and how you can pace with a comfortable match. You may even be able to notice just how your client's hips, thighs, knees and shins relaxed and how your hips and legs are now releasing into a deeper level of relaxation.

As you drift off into the world of deep, meaningful possibility, just take a deep breath in . . . then let that breath out with a sigh and allow yourself the experience of your favorite meditation or place for relaxation. Imagine the possibility of building a garden in your mind . . . a beautiful, peaceful place with the fresh scent and calming sounds of nature all around. Imagine the taste of deep, deep relaxation moving into your mind as you gain a flavor for the experience. You are naturally clearing the filters of your mind's eye to see the golden shaft of the sun beaming down and into the top of your head, burning away any negative thoughts, beliefs or influences. Allow the delicate, white clouds to float overhead . . . representing your true self image. Right here and right now you are establishing the truth for you, and for every one of your clients . . . that every day and in every way we learn and discover just what we need the most.

As the days in your mind become weeks . . . and the weeks transform into months . . . and the months flow into years, imagine the vastness of a blue sky in your perfect place of relaxation. Notice how the blue sky extends in all directions . . . adding to your mind an expanded view of the session you have just completed. From that place, drift off into a dream where you can create the possibility of going back through time to the very beginning for you . . . taking the information you experienced today along with you. Can you feel how your past is being upgraded from what you have discovered today? . . . And how you are now reinforcing your connection to the therapeutic mind?

I'm going to pause now. This quiet space is for you to allow your mind to move through time in the direction of your goals . . . at times you may be moving through the days and weeks of the past . . . at other times you may be mentally reviewing the future . . . making all the changes and enhancements that are needed to mentally, physically and emotionally re-charge the therapeutic mind . . .

You will have all the time you need to finish the sequence of thoughts that will structure positive and resourceful sessions and bring about the results your future clients desire . . . Then, and only then, will your eyes open and at that point you can return to the room and full conscious awareness . . . refreshed, revitalized and anticipating your next opportunity to help another person as you help yourself.

"If you had faith even as small as a tiny mustard seed nothing would be impossible."

MATTHEW 17:20 LB

Note to Therapists:
I hope that you will always remember that practice is the very best teacher of all. When performing therapy with other people, you cannot do any harm as long as your intentions are for helping them and you are moving in the direction of accomplishing their goals. Always move with ecology—staying in tune with the thoughts, feelings and ambitions of your clients. You will indeed lead them to just where they want to be.

If you would like more information or some working tools for Psycho-Linguistics, we do offer tapes and transcripts in the areas of Smoking Cessation, Weight Control, Insomnia, Sports Improvement and more. We also offer training in Psycho-Linguistics and a Board certified hypnotherapy certification program. Internships are available at our corporate headquarters (interview required). Feel free to contact one of our offices or affiliates for a free brochure.

Corporate Headquarters
Positive Changes Hypnosis
Patrick K. Porter, Ph.D
Al Stalcup, Ch.t.
Co-Directors
256 North Witchduck Road ste A
Virginia Beach, Virginia 23462
(804) 499-5097 fax (804) 499-6708
Email pch@livnet.com

Positive Changes-LeHigh Valley
Cynthia Fertal, Director
Bethlehem, Pennsylvania
610-691-5541

Positive Changes of Las Vegas
Jon-Terrance Diegel, Director
Las Vegas, Nevada
(702) 735-7911

Positive Changes of Portland
Richard Anrich, Director
Portland, Oregon
(503) 626-6577

Positive Changes of Dayton
Barb & Ron Scandlin
Dayton, Ohio
(513)298-4939

Positive Changes of Phoenix
Normand Charette, Director
Phoenix, Arizona
(602) 978-9559

Positive Changes of the
Capital District
Carl Utter, Director
Burnt Hills, New York
518-399-1300

Internationally:
Positive Changes of Vernon
Leigh Perry, Director
Vernon, British Columbia, Canada
604-545-4377

McCann Consultancy Ltd
Jane McCann or Mary Henry
PO Box 27106
Wellington,New Zealand
64-4-801-8082

Anglo-American Books
Martin Roberts, Ph.D
Underwood,St.Clears, Carmarthen
Dyfed, U.K. SA33 4NE
44-994-230400

Index

BIBLIOGRAPHY

1. Andreas, Steve and Connirae. Change Your Mind--And Keep the Change. Moab, Utah: Real People Press, 1987.

2. Alcoholics Anonymous World Services, Inc., Alcoholics Anonymous. 3rd Edition, 1976.

3. Bandler, Leslie Cameron, et al. Know How. San Rafael, California: FuturePace, Inc. , 1985.

4. Bandler, Richard and John Grinder. Frogs Into Princes. Moab, Utah: Real People Press, 1979.

5. Braid, James, M.R.C.S.E., C.M.W.S&c. Neurypnology. Edinburgh, Scotland: John Churchill, 1843.

6. Dilts, Robert; et al. Neuro Linguistic Programming: Volume I. Cupertino, California: Meta Publications, 1980.

7. Erickson, Milton H., MD. Life Reframing in Hypnosis. New York, New York: Irvington Publishers, Inc., 1985.

8. Erickson, Milton H., MD. Time Distortion in Hypnosis. New York, New York: Irvington Publishers, Inc., 1982.

9. Erickson, Milton H., MD. Experiencing Hypnosis. New York, New York: Irvington Publishers, 1981.

10. Gilligan, Stephen G. Therapeutic Trances -- The Cooperation Principle in Ericksonian Hypnotherapy, Brunner/Mazel, Inc., 1987

11. James, Tad and Wyatt Woodsmall. Time Line Therapy and the Basis of Personality, Cupertino, California: Meta Publications, 1988.

12. Kostere, Kim and Linda Malatesta. <u>Get the Results You Want: Neuro-Linguistic Programming</u>. Portland, Oregon: Metamorphous Press, Inc., 1985.

13. Metos, Thomas H. <u>The Human Mind--How We Think and Learn</u>. Franklin Watts, 1990.

14. Rushkoff, Douglas and Patrick Wells. <u>Free Rides -- How to Get High Without Drugs</u>. New York, New York: Bantam Doubleday Dell Publishing, 1991

15. Weitzenhoffer, Andre' M. <u>General Techniques of Hypnotism</u>. Grune & Stratton, Inc., 1957.

About The Cover Artist:

Sam Davis Johnson is an illustrator from Lexington, Kentucky. The covers for Dr. Porter's books were created with airbrush, colored pencil, pen & ink and brush techniques.

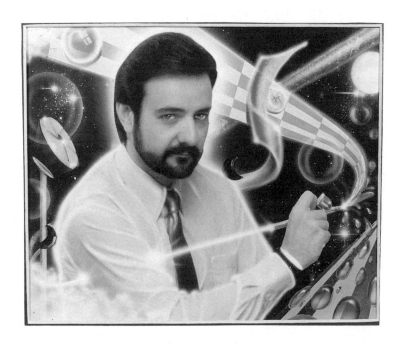

Mr. Johnson's studio, ABS Airbrush Illustration & Design is engaged in artwork for the advertising and publishing industry. For more information: 606-273-7075

Dear Student of the Mind:

As you know, today's modern technology is advancing so rapidly that what is new and innovative today will be obsolete a year from now. Is humankind keeping up? The truth is some people are, but many more are not. We are all moving; some people are going forward, some backward, and many are going wherever advertisers tell them to go!

The mission of the *Positive Changes Network* is to give all people, from every walk of life, the opportunity to awaken their minds to the possibility that there is another possibility; it exists in the limitlessness of their potential. It is our strong belief that everyone is imbued with the ability to shine and the *Network* and *Awaken the Genius Project* are designed to give each individual the tools to awaken that 90% of un-used mind potential so their genius can be radiant!

Is the opportunity as an *Awaken Your Genius!* Workshop Leader and/or as a certified hypnotherapist for you? It is if you want to be on the leading edge of mind technology . . . if you have a desire to help people out of the prison of their conscious thinking and into that *other-than-conscious* level of their mind — the one that exists outside of time and knows no restrictions or limitations.

I invite you to read through the following pages to help you better understand the *Network* and *Awaken the Genius Project* and what it will mean to you. It is my sincere hope that you will discover a comfortable blending of your dreams and ours. On the back page you will find a form for expressing interest in the project. We will be pleased to contact you with information on training in your area.

Yours In Genius,

Patrick Porter
Patrick Porter

"BECOME A TRAINED HYPNOTIST!"

Learn the techniques that have helped thousands of people to stop smoking, lose weight, overcome fears, gain self-confidence, and more...

The Positive Changes Hypnotist Certification Training (resulting in CHT) is so much more than a typical hypnotherapy certification. The initial training includes today's most advanced technology such as Neuro-Linguistic Programming, Ericksonian Hypnosis and Psycho-Linguistics. From there, Positive Changes' support is continuous as you become an integral part of our network of highly-skilled, super-charged hypnosis professionals (just like you) who want to help hundreds of people and make a more than comfortable living. Positive Changes Hypnosis' mission statement, *"To activate the planet's genius one person at a time through the re-empowerment of the individual, so that each person's life, and the lives of those they love, will be positively changed forever,"* becomes more than just words.

Are you ready to step up to your next level of learning?

Once trained, you will be eligible to participate in our **Positive Changes' Hypnosis Practice-Builder Program.** You will have access to proven marketing strategies to assertively promote your services, including innovative newspaper, radio, television and other media. You will be a respected asset to your community as you provide a successful alternative for smoking cessation and weight control as well as other wellness programs for psychosomatic disorders. Once trained you will be highly skilled and feel confident in offering quality, one-on-one, completely confidential hypnotic sessions, along with no-risk guarantees for weight loss, smoking cessation, and more.

Can you imagine becoming the entrepreneur you dreamed of being, but with the full support of a thirty-year old company? With the **Positive Changes Hypnosis' Practice-Builder Program** you will have 100% financial control of your business and never pay a "franchise fee." Once a member of the Positive Changes' Network, you will have on-going training and support.

If you're at all interested in becoming a certified professional hypnotist... if you want to get astounding client results, earn more than you ever dreamed possible, and receive accolades from your colleagues and friends, simply turn the page to find out more. Then call us toll free at **1-800-880-0436** for your FREE information kit.

"SKYROCKET YOUR EXISTING HYPNOSIS PRACTICE WITH POSITIVE CHANGES HYPNOSIS' PRACTICE-BUILDER PROGRAM!"

Positive Changes has made tremendous progress since developing our current strategies in 1986. We accomplish what most hypnotists are unable to do, that is, make hypnosis a profitable business. The reasons for our success:

We have minimized the drawbacks of most hypnosis practices, such as determining your clientele and how to bring them into the office. This is done through our successful advertising and development of phone procedures that work.

At Positive Changes we have proven formulas for success. We have learned what works in the advertising arena. An advertising expert once said that when you first start advertising you use about 50% of your budget before you find out what works for you. At Positive Changes, we eliminate that potentially wasted expenditure with our fully developed, time-tested, and proven advertising formula that typically brings in hundreds of new clients.

We qualify our clients by telephone. We train you to handle all prospective clients through proven telephone strategies that greatly reduce your time on the telephone.

We have developed programs that get client results. At Positive Changes, our programs revolve around hypnosis. However, with Psycho-Linguistics, we are in no way limited to hypnosis alone. We also use the advanced technology of bio-feed-in equipment. Training is continuous and our programs are updated regularly.

Just read the informational communiqué from hypnotist Normand Charette on the next page...

Since Implementing the Positive Changes System, I Went From Working Out of My Home to a 2,000 Square Foot Prestige Facility!

— *Normand Charette, Phoenix, Arizona*

Dr. Patrick Porter's hypnosis practice has been acclaimed as the largest and most successful in the world. Now he wants to send you complete details on how you, too, can take your practice to new heights, attracting thousands of new hypnosis clients and achieving astounding client results... Without knowing <u>anything</u> about advertising, selling or even running a front office!

If you ever wanted to "jump start" your hypnosis practice and begin earning many times what you're earning now, helping hundreds more people at the same time...

If you've ever wanted to have all the work of marketing and advertising your services done by someone else, using dozens of ads and other marketing vehicles that are proven to work before you ever try them -- I urge you to call for a detailed information package about an exciting new program designed specifically for those of us in the hypnosis field who want to make a better than decent income, doing the work we love to do.

A proven system that generates results!

Over the past two and a half years, Dr. Patrick Porter has built his own hypnosis practice to unprecedented levels... and his clients have experienced astounding results. His clients are so happy they regularly send friends, family and colleagues to his practice. And they write testimonials he can use to convince others to try hypnosis services.

He's helped a handful of other hypnotists around the country (like me) achieve the same kinds of results and earn the same kind of income. Now, he's packaged everything he's ever used to build his own practice, into a six-month training program that will build your practice to astounding new levels in just a few short months.

Ads, Scripts, Letters, Forms... Everything You'll Ever Need

The program includes three days of intense training in Virginia Beach, VA plus six months of follow-up consultation by phone to be sure you're experiencing maximum growth.

<u>Plus</u>, you get *everything* you need to succeed in the hypnosis field including: proven newspaper ads that bring in *hundreds* (not dozens) of prospects, training on how to turn 80 percent or more of these prospects into eager clients, proven hypnosis scripts that get maximum results, over 100 audio-hypnosis cassettes, reproducible front office forms, manuals for giving public seminars and workshops, sample new client kits, ancillary products your clients will buy, testimonial videos for your waiting room or lobby, physician referral programs, an intern training program... and more!

Call 1-800-880-0436 For Your Free Info Kit

Your information package includes an audio tape of an exciting conference call Dr. Porter held recently to announce his Practice Builder Program. Dozens of hypnotists were on the line, asking tough questions... and getting straight answers. There were even a handful of hypnotists online (like me) who are *already* using Dr. Porter's system, discussing in specific detail the exact strategies we're using to earn $8,000 or more a week and up to $50,000 or more every month. There's no cost or obligation to receive the info kit and audiotape. The program starts with a three-day training weekend. Space is strictly limited. Call for dates and locations. **Call 1-800-880-0436 for your info kit *today*.**

-- Normand Charette

Conduct Your Own Awaken the Genius Seminars!

The *Awaken Your Genius!* Seminar is an experiential program; meaning it involves learning through seeing, hearing, doing, and integrating. The program uses the cutting-edge technology outlined in Dr. Patrick Porter's book **Awaken the Genius** and features a powerful synthesis of *Psycho-Linguistics (the language of the mind), Neuro-Linguistic Programming (NLP)*, guided imagery and actual exercises. As a seminar leader of *Awaken Your Genius!,* you will be guiding the participants to a greater understanding of:

> *** The stuff "genius" is made of –**
> **and how to get it.**
> *** Their own unlimited potential –**
> **and how to recognize it.**
> *** The magic of the brain/mind –**
> **and how to balance the power.**
> *** The "Other-Than-Conscious-Mind" --**
> **and how to activate it.**
> *** Learning Preferences –**
> **and how to integrate them.**
> *** Their relationship to the past –**
> **and how to transform it.**

The power of the seminar resides in integration. Each dynamic piece is integrated through self-discovery exercises and powerful guided imageries that awaken, activate and inspire *the other-than-conscious* mind. The seminar is filled with adventure and excitement. Participants frequently experience the *"ah-ha"* response by recognizing the inherent truths in each new discovery.

As an *Awaken Your Genius!* Seminar leader, you have the opportunity to be on the leading edge of mind technology, as well as facilitate these breakthrough changes in people's lives. After completing the training, you will be entitled to 100% of the profits from the seminars you present.

To learn more about how you can begin conducting **Awaken the Genius** seminars in your home town, or add them to your existing training or consulting repertoire, call (757) 499-5097. You'll receive complete materials including a detailed facilitator's manual, individual participant workbooks and popular **Awaken the Genius** booklets your workshop attendees need to succeed.

ORDER FORM

☎ Telephone orders: **Call 1-800-880-0436** *(orders only)*

✉ Postal orders: **ATG Publishing, c/o 309 Aragona Blvd., 102-712, Virginia Beach, Virginia, PZ/C [23462]. USA**

Please send the following products/information. I understand that I may return any products for a full refund — for any reason, no questions asked.

❑ I want to know more about the **Positive Changes Hypnosis Practice-Builder Program**. Please send my **FREE** Info Kit and Audio Preview.

❑ I'm interested in the **Positive Changes Hypnosis and Psycho-Linguistics Certification Training**. Please send **FREE** information.

❑ Please send **FREE** information on **Awaken the Genius** Seminar Leadership.

Quantity

_____ **Psycho-Linguistics** book $14.95 ea.

_____ **Psycho-Linguistics** Audio Book (unabridged) $29.95 ea.

_____ Personal Evolution **"Success!"** Tape Set $16.00 ea.

_____ Personal Evolution **"Stop Smoking!"** Tape Set $16.00 ea.

_____ Personal Evolution **"Weight Control!"** Tape Set $16.00 ea.

_____ **Awaken the Genius** book $14.95 ea.

_____ **Awaken the Genius** Audio Book (abridged) $16.00 ea.

_____ **Six Secrets of G.E.N.I.U.S.** book $7.95 ea.

_____ **Adventures in Self-Discovery** 4-processes $16.00 ea.

_____ **Adventures in Accelerated Learning** 4-processes $16.00 ea.

_____ **Hypno-Specialist Kit I** (*Hypno-Transcripts for weight loss & stop smoking*) $77.00.

_____ **Hypno-Specialist Kit II** (*Specialized Hypno-Transcripts*) $77.00 ea.

_____ Order **Specialist Kit I** and receive **Kit II** 1/2 price. $115.50 for both!

Name: _____

Address: _____

City: _____ State: _____ Zip: _____-____

Phone: (   ) _____-_____

Shipping: Book Rate: $3.00 for the first book and 75 cents for each additional book. (Surface shipping may take three to four weeks.) Air Mail: $3.50 per book

Payment: ❑Check ❑ Visa ❑MasterCard ❑Amex ❑Discover

Card number: _____ Exp. date: ____/____

Name on card: _____ Signature : _____